Profiles of SAINTS

CORNELIO FABRO

Publications of the Cornelio Fabro Cultural Project

Introduction to Cornelio Fabro
By Elvio C. Fontana
Studia Fabriana, Vol. 1: Cornelio Fabro, Essential Thinker

SELECTED WORKS OF CORNELIO FABRO

Vol. 1: Selected Articles on Metaphysics and Participation
With Introduction by John F. Wippel

Vol. 9: God, An Introduction to Problems in Theology
With Introduction by Michael J. Dodds

FORTHCOMING

Vol. 2: Selected Articles on Søren Kierkegaard
Vol. 3: Selected Articles on Atheism and Freedom
Vol. 4: The Metaphysical Notion of Participation
Vol. 5: Phenomenology of Perception
Vol. 6: Perception and Thought
Vol. 10: The Soul, Introduction to the Problem of Man
Vol. 12: Participation and Causality
Vol. 13: God in Exile, Introduction to Modern Atheism
Vol. 17: The Anthropological Turn of Karl Rahner
Vol. 18: Prayer in Modern Thought
Vol. 19: Introduction to St. Thomas
Vol. 20: Reflections on Freedom
Vol. 21: Gemma Galgani, Witness to the Supernatural
Introduction to Søren Kierkegaard
Moments of the Spirit Vols. 1 and 2
Cornelio Fabro: Biographical Profile
Commentary on the Our Father
Sunday Gospels

Profiles of
SAINTS
CORNELIO FABRO

Translated by
Giulio Silano
University of St. Michael's College
University of Toronto

Edited by
Nathaniel Dreyer
Cornelio Fabro Cultural Project

IVE Press

Edited by the Cornelio Fabro Cultural Project
of the Institute of the Incarnate Word

Cover Design
    © 2019 by IVE Press, Chillum, MD
    Institute of the Incarnate Word, Inc.
    All rights reserved

    © 2019 by Cornelio Fabro Cultural Project
    All rights reserved

Intellectual Property: Province of the Sacred Heart, Italy
                              Congregation of the Sacred Stigmata

Originally published in Italian as *Profili di Santi*, 1957
Reprinted and edited in Opere Complete, Volume 14, by EDIVI, 2008

First English translation published 2019

BWGRKL, BWGRKN, and BWGRKI [Greek] PostScript® Type 1 and TrueType fonts Copyright ©1994–2013 BibleWorks, LLC. All rights reserved. These Biblical Greek fonts are used with permission and are from BibleWorks (www.bibleworks.com). Please comply with all applicable copyright legislation.

E-mail: fabroproject@corneliofabro.org

www.corneliofabro.org/en
www.ivepress.org

ISBN: 978-1-939018-85-4

Library of Congress Control Number: 2018933674

Printed in the United States of America

Contents

Preface	VII
Introduction – Fr. Joseph C. Henchey, CSS	IX
Abbreviations	XVII
FOREWORD	1
ST. THOMAS AQUINAS – OR ON ITALIAN GENTILITY	3
CONVERSATIONS ON ST. JOHN OF GOD	9
EDITH STEIN – FROM PHILOSOPHY TO MARTYRDOM	15
BARTOLOMEA CAPITANIO – THE LITTLE TEACHER OF LOVERE	21
VINCENZA GEROSA – THE LADY OF CHARITY	31
MARIA GORETTI – CONSCIOUS OF INNOCENCE	37
THE LITTLE FLOWERS OF SISTER BERTILLA	43
"POOR GEMMA" – ON THE FIFTIETH ANNIVERSARY OF HER DEATH (1953)	49
THE HUMILITY AND GREATNESS OF POPE SARTO	55
THE "LETTERS" OF ST. PIUS X	69
THE IMMACULATE IN THE HISTORY OF THE WORLD	91

Preface

The Cornelio Fabro Cultural Project is pleased to present this translation into English of *Profili di Santi* (Segni [RM]: EDIVI, 2008). Congratulations and thanks are in order to the translator of this volume, Giulio Silano, Professor of the University of St. Michael's College and the University of Toronto.

This translation has been made to follow Fabro's original text as closely as possible. However, in order to make the text more accessible to English readers, the following changes have been made:

— Regarding the names of persons, where Fabro only gave a surname, the first name has also been included when useful.

— Long quotations have been separated from the paragraph and indented to distinguish Fabro's words from the quoted material.

— Where a citation was missing, the source or a comparable reference has been provided when possible. For quotations from texts available in English, the published English translations have been used and cited. For certain quotations, other useful English references have been included where no exact English translation is available.

— This text uses two sets of footnotes. The first set, designated with Arabic numerals, are Fabro's notes. While keeping Fabro's style, complete names and titles have been given for abbreviations uncommon in English. For other abbreviations, the English equivalents have been used.

— The second set of footnotes, indicated with letters, are notes from the editor. These include corrections to any errors or discrepancies in the original document, citations as mentioned above, and other relevant remarks. Occasional notes from the editor are designated with [Ed.].

The Project thanks Fr. Joseph C. Henchey, CSS, for his Introduction to this volume, as well as Sr. María de La Salette Casariego, SSVM, whose keen editorial work for the 2008 Italian edition of this text can only be partially appreciated in this translation. Lastly, a word of gratitude to those who assisted in preparing this book for publication, especially the religious of the Institute of the Incarnate Word and the Servants of the Lord and the Virgin of Matará.

Fr. Nathaniel Dreyer, IVE
May 2, 2019

Introduction

FR. JOSEPH C. HENCHEY, CSS

It is a great honor for me to offer this Introduction to the English translation of *Profiles of Saints*, one of Fr. Cornelio Fabro's many books. I must quickly say, however, that I feel more than a little out of my comfort zone in this undertaking because Fr. Fabro and I are in quite different leagues! He was a prolific writer and original thinker, one we could easily call a true philosopher; whereas my work has focused on teaching.

I met Fr. Fabro when I was a young man studying in Rome and we continued a fraternal association until his death forty years later. Twenty years my senior, he was renowned for his intellectual prowess and his contributions to philosophy, theology, and spirituality. I was also touched by the attention he gave our younger confreres in his later years, both in lively conversation at table and during recreation. Thus, it gives me tremendous pleasure that this new translation of his work will not only make it possible for our Stigmatine confrere to be even more widely read, but hopefully might make some small assistance, to help him to be even better known.

Notwithstanding the differences in our work, I believe I have something particular to offer in this Introduction because Fr. Fabro and I have shared the same charism. We lived as confreres in the Congregation of the Sacred Stigmata, the Stigmatines, and share a devotion to St. Gaspar Bertoni, priest of Verona, and founder of our Congregation. We share the ideals of our Congregation, inspired from the earliest years of our formation to evangelize with the word of God—*quocumque*—anywhere in the diocese and the world, in accordance with the needs of the Church.

I am now older by four years than Fr. Fabro was when he died († May 4, 1995) and during these twilight years of my own life, I have had the opportunity to read much of Fr. Fabro's work, some of it for the second time, and some of it for the first. Reading him has allowed me to revisit the philosophical foundation of St. Thomas Aquinas and to discover Søren Kierkegaard (favorably mentioned by St. John Paul II in his *Fides et Ratio*), a distinct gap in my own knowledge. In preparing to speak at the Symposium in Washington, D.C. honoring Fr. Cornelio Fabro and his life's work a few years ago, I also had the chance to review the few, but important, essays he wrote on our founder, St. Gaspar Bertoni. This range of reading has had a significant impact on me and has given me a vantage point from which I can see something of the arc of Fr. Fabro's own intellectual and spiritual development.

Simply put, Fr. Fabro was a *forerunner* in the articulation of the concept of "participation" in St. Thomas, a *teacher* of the notion of "contemporaneity" explored by Kierkegaard, and a sincere *devotee* of the spirituality of the saints including that of St. Gaspar Bertoni whose decades of suffering worked with that grace by which he grew in unity with Christ until the hour of his death.

We could consider Fabro's writings to be of three classes—philosophy, theology, and spirituality—and he has given significant written contributions to each.[1] The book translated here, *Profiles of Saints*, is one I would put squarely in the third class, and in it he shows how these saints lived out the ideas of "participation" and "contemporaneity" which he would profoundly study for his whole life.

St. Thomas and "Participation"

Fr. Fabro wrote his doctoral thesis on St. Thomas's concept of "participation," and because he continued to revise this work over many

---

[1] See the following volumes from Fabro's Opere Complete (OC) published by EDIVI. For Thomistic works on participation: *La nozione metafisica di partecipazione*, OC 3; *Partecipazione e causalità*, OC 19. For modern philosophical works, esp. on modern atheism (*God in Exile*): OC 21. For Kierkegaardian scholarship: OC 8–11. For spiritual writings on St. Gemma Galgani: *Gemma Galgani, Testimone del soprannaturale* (Rome: CIPI, 1989); *Breviario d'amore* (Lucca: Ed. Eco, 1999); *Lettere su Santa Gemma* (Segni: EDIVI, 2013). For devotional writings on St. Gaspar Bertoni, Stigmatine Founder, see the works listed in: Joseph C. Henchey, "Father Cornelio Fabro: Stigmatine – Devotee of His Founder," *Studia Fabriana* 1 (2017): 29.

years, it is clear that he was captivated by this subject and he broke new ground in it as his studies evolved.²

Fr. Fabro's understanding of "participation" begins with the idea that as God operates in all things, he is the universal First Cause of all beings in action. Human creatures share in this causality by having been created by him, but also because God's Only Son became "a partaker of our human nature," thereby not only renewing the whole human race, but giving each of us the innate power to become *partakers of his divinity* (cf. Jn 1; 2 Pt 1:4). Through the grace of Christ, we, too, are called to become true and responsible *instruments of God's will*.

Yet, between God and all that is created, there is a far greater dissimilarity than similarity,³ insofar as some scholars hold that "being" in God is *not-univocal with that in his creatures*, but rather an analogy based on participation. Fr. Fabro beautifully develops the theme of "supernatural participation" in the "elevation to grace and glory," showing that since we are made to the image and likeness of God, we are still "restless" creatures. The human soul is naturally capable of God, but we are not God, and our human natures are naturally oriented toward him, but we are not God! As our natural inclination toward God couples with our natural desire for happiness, our human minds are motivated to strive for the Ultimate Truth and our wills to reach for the most sublime Good. Yet because we cannot completely achieve these heights, either on our own or during this life on earth, we experience an "interior tension," a "propensity towards him," which unsettles us and, if we will allow God to work on us, this tension can spur us on a lifelong growth in faith.

Thus, our "participation" in the divine nature is a basic reality of our human being. We are created with a passive *obediential potency* which is activated in response to the First Cause, to God himself. Living lives of faith, we grow and participate more and more deeply in the Divine Intellect and Will, gradually approaching the very nature of the Triune God (cf. 2 Pt 1:4). Jesus Christ is joined to each human being (GS 22) yet we remain unfinished until such time, as Jesus says, *"When I am raised up, I will 'draw' all to myself"* (Jn 12:32).

---

² Cornelio Fabro, *La nozione metafisica di partecipazione secondo s. Tommaso d'Aquino*, 2nd ed., revised and augmented (Turin: SEI, 1950), 299–331. There is evidence that this idea was pondered throughout his entire life. Cf. OC 3 and 19.

³ Cf. IV Lateran Council, Denzinger-Schönmetzer, *Enchiridion Symbolorum* (1965), no. 805.

Kierkegaard and "Contemporaneity"

"Contemporaneity" is simply another way of saying "*In Christ Jesus,*" but such a profound idea is not so easily explained. St. Paul tried valiantly, often resorting to repurposing old words or inventing new ones to express the ineffable union of Christians with Christ and in Christ.

To illustrate the problem, below is a list of such verbs as found in the Vulgate.[4] Our understanding of the idea "*In Christ Jesus*" is further complicated by the difficulties of translating any of these words into the modern languages. This can often be done only with a clumsy re-expression or circumlocution. Here are some of those words translated into English and as we can see, sometimes the attempt to bring greater clarity results in greater obscurity.

Latin Verb	Vulgate	English Translation
compati	Rom 8:17 1 Cor 12:26	to suffer with him
simul crucifigi	Rom 6:6	to be crucified with him
configi cruci	Gal 2:20	
commori	2 Tm 2:11 cf. 2 Cor 7:3	to die with him
consepeliri	Rom 6:4 Col 2:12	to be buried with him
conresuscitare	Eph 2:6 passive: Col 2:12, 3:1	to rise from the dead with him
simul vivere cum	Rom 6:8	to live with him
convivere	2 Tm 2:11	
convivificare	Eph 2:5 Col 2:13	to be made alive with him

---

[4] Ferdinand Prat, *The Theology of St. Paul*, trans. John L. Stoddard, vol. 2 (Westminster, MD: Newman, 1927), 18 ff.

Latin Verb	Vulgate	English Translation
configurari	Phil 3:10	to share his form
conglorificari	Rom 8:17	to share his glory
consedere facere	Eph 2:6	to sit with him
conregnare	2 Tm 2:12 cf. 1 Cor 4:8	to reign with him
conformis	Rom 8:29 Phil 3:21	to be conformed with him
complantatus	Rom 6:5	united with him
coheres	Rom 8:17 Eph 3:6	coheir with him
comparticeps	Eph 3:6; 5:7	co-partner
concorporalis	Eph 3:6	concorporate
coaedificari	Eph 2:22	built together
constructus	Eph 2:21 Col 2:19	structured together
compactus	Eph 4:16	joined together
connexus	Eph 4:16	

By virtue of his studies on Kierkegaard, Fr. Fabro ultimately taught that "*In Christ Jesus*" expresses a "contemporary presence, participation of believers, of the faithful, of each of us, in the Paschal Mystery," as in the sufferings of Christ.[5] It is meant as a kind of existential mystical continuation, a life shared in his Death and in his Resurrection offered once and for all for the redemption of the world (cf. Rom 4:25). Thus for

---

[5] Cf. excerpts from Barnabas Mary Ahern, "The Fellowship of His Sufferings (Phil 3:10)," doctoral thesis, *Catholic Biblical Quarterly* 22 (1960): 1–32.

all time there will be a "contemporaneity of repentance and of expiation" for all the sins in the entire world as the faithful are being transformed, conformed to the Paschal Mystery of the Lord. Because we faithful participate in the Lord's ongoing and active reparation for sin in our own time on earth, we all participate in the eternal salvation of the world.

Maurizio Schoepflin has succinctly treated this idea in *Fabro nei suoi scritti spirituali* [Fabro in his spiritual writings] and his perspective is well worth noting here.[6] He states that Fr. Fabro understood this "contemporaneity," not as the ongoing process of "updating" the Church, nor as the effort of rendering Christianity "actual," but rather as a philosophical-theological concept, a "prophetic [*metaphysical*] moment," bringing eternity into time, joining the "today" with every "tomorrow" as we commit to a lifetime of strenuous effort to imitate, copy, and "draw" a portrait of Him in our own lives. Whoever makes such an effort to imitate Him is "contemporary" to Him, in Fr. Fabro's view, and this is an essential urgency of the Christian life in our time. It is *this* day, and every day, we are urged to copy the Model, and to imitate Christ in our daily crosses.

Fr. Fabro and the Extraordinary Sufferings of the Saints: A Participation in Christ's Stigmata: Making the Sufferings of Christ "Contemporary"

Fr. Fabro's inspiring *Profiles of Saints* was originally published in 1957 as a collection of several articles published earlier in the 1950's, and then republished as part of a two-volume set entitled *Momenti dello Spirito*[7] or "Moments of the Spirit." Along with great moments in the Church, inspired by the Holy Spirit (such as the "Better World Movement," the Vatican II era) Fr. Fabro considered the saints as more than individual people, but also as "moments" of the Holy Spirit. We need only to think of St. Pius X, St. John Paul II, and St. Teresa of Calcutta to see how the Holy Spirit used their individual lives and sufferings to spark great moments of faith.

Fr. Fabro's *Profiles of Saints* encourages us to see that the lives of the martyrs, mystics, and saints are specific examples of the timeless goal

---

[6] Cf. Maurizio Schoepflin, *Fabro nei suoi scritti spirituali* (Segni: EDIVI, 2008), 39–45.
[7] Cornelio Fabro, *Momenti dello Spirito* (Assisi: Ed. Sala Francescana di Cultura, 1982). Part I of Volume I is entitled "Words and Deeds." Part II is "The Adventure of Freedom." Part III is the *Profiles*, including the first ten saints pondered by Fr. Fabro.

of unity in Christ. They taught by example, living in ways that contradicted the norm of their own times and indeed still contradict our own (cf. Wis 2). Their examples bring traditional catechetical teaching to life as they show us time after time how to *"put on the mind of Christ Jesus"* (cf. Phil 2:5) and how to pattern ourselves more closely on him.

These saints accepted Jesus Christ as an *"Exemplary Cause,"* as St. Thomas Aquinas put it. They deeply understood Jesus as a *Model* to be emulated with God's grace, a *Copy* to be imitated, and a *Portrait* to be drawn in their own lives. As we read Fr. Fabro's descriptions, we are able to observe how they "copied" Christ in their day and age and having done so, it becomes possible for us to see how to do the same in our own. One after another, Fr. Fabro lets them invite us to hold up Christ as our "mirror" too, that by seeing him, we might trace the more his image in ourselves and ourselves in him as we strive to make our lifelong response to the graces of Baptism. As we do, we gradually become graced "epistles" (cf. 2 Cor 3:2) ourselves of the Most Beloved, Only Begotten Word of God to the world around us.

Furthermore, these saints show us that such an imitation is, in fact, an expansion of our experience of life, allowing us to enter into a *"new space for human freedom."* These saints, people we might call "events" of sacred history, reveal *a providential encounter between divine freedom and human liberty in a particular time and place*: The God-Man-Redeemer meets sinful humanity in an ongoing experience of redemption.

With these ideas in mind, we realize that when we pattern ourselves deeply on Christ, truly sharing in his personal mission (cf. Jn 20), his sufferings become "contemporary"; they become a reality "of our time" as they are of his eternal Time. In this instant, in our lives, in this opportune present moment (*kairos*), Providence is unfolding in just the way God intends it. *Now* is the hour! *This* is the acceptable time! And so we pray ever more ardently, "Give us *this* day," "Pray for us *now* and at the hour of our death," and most profoundly of all, "*This* is the day the Lord has made, let us rejoice and be glad in it!"

"*This is the day the Lord has made, let us rejoice and be glad in it*" is a perfect expression of the spirituality of St. Gaspar Bertoni, priest of Verona, founder of the Stigmatine Congregation, that Fr. Fabro and I share in common. As with so many saints before him, St. Gaspar experienced God's grace every day in the Eucharist and that grace allowed him to deeply unite his own sufferings with those our Lord Jesus Christ suffered in the Sacred Stigmata.

Many of the 76 years of St. Gaspar Bertoni's life were spent in atrocious physical and spiritual suffering. But through God's Providence and his devotion to the Eucharist, his suffering accompanied, elevated, and permeated his spiritual growth. St. Gaspar teaches us how much the burdensome crosses we carry moment to moment must also be lived through and nourished by that Most Precious Sacrament.

In the entry he made in his *Spiritual Journal* on September 17, 1808 when he was just 31 years old, we can glimpse something of the spirituality developing in him and which for us Stigmatines has made him a saint for the ages:

> *Meditation. Death. The past is no more. The future has not yet arrived. Only the present is here. And it is in my hands. Let me live day after day, or rather from morning to midday and from midday to evening. Let me do every single thing with all possible perfection. Perhaps I will have no more time in which to glorify God.*[8]

"*By his wounds, ours are healed!*" (Is 53:5; 1 Pt 2:2 ff.)

---

[8] Gaspar Bertoni, *The Spiritual Journal [Memoriale Privato]: 1808–1813*, trans. Giancarlo Mittempergher (1992), electronic ed., September 17, 1808, p. 53, no. 49.

Abbreviations

ST   *Summa Theologiae*, Thomas Aquinas

JP   *Søren Kierkegaard's Journals and Papers*, edited and translated by H. V. Hong and E. H. Hong, 7 volumes, Bloomington: Indiana University Press, 1967–1978

References followed by volume (I–VII) and serial entry number

Pap.   *Søren Kierkegaards Papirer*, edited by P. A. Heiberg, V. Kuhr, and E. Torsting, 2nd enlarged edition by N. Thulstrup, index by N. J. Cappelørn, 16 volumes, Copenhagen: Gyldendal, 1909–1978

References followed by volume (I–XVI), tome (if any) in superscript, section (A, B, C), and serial entry number

Foreword

I ask the forgiveness of the dear saints in this little volume for the presumption that I have shown in writing about their lives; I beg pardon from the reader for the little, exceedingly little, which they will find here regarding the greatness of these souls who beautify the City of God. But these saints now see in the light of God the mission of example and consolation of their suffering within the Mystical Body of Christ. They will certainly exhibit a liberal and fraternal condescension toward some poor brother who, yet a pilgrim, tries to approach the drama of their earthly lives in order to glean for himself some glimmer of truth, some small drop of joy, so as not to despair over his own misery.

These writings, which are tied together only by the luminous thread of divine grace that is powerful in the weak, first appeared as commemorations in the Vatican journal *Ecclesia*. Now, with only slight alterations they are presented in collection.

Rome, Feast of All Saints, 1955

The Author

St. Thomas Aquinas

OR ON ITALIAN GENTILITY

William of Tocco, the official biographer for St. Thomas's cause for canonization, writes that Br. Thomas was tall in stature and wonderfully proportioned in his members; he had blond hair and his face was tanned by the sun. The subtle line of his lips betrayed both his goodness and his firmness; his eyes showed clarity and penetrating calmness. These reflecting and searching eyes are truly characteristic of the ancient representations of St. Thomas. Completely abstracted from the surrounding world, they seem to fix upon an aim distant yet present to the contemplating spirit, not as if lost in a dream, but as if being lifted up wholly in the ardor of a striking truth. Thomas is seized by a specific difficulty, pondering a specific mystery . . . and then, behold . . . the light of new knowledge flashes victorious in his spirit. Yet another moment and that silent mouth will open and convey to us the treasure uncovered, or else his slightly raised hand will write down his new intuition in the open tome before him.

The saint had a delicate, sensitive constitution, very receptive to joy and sorrow, and a rare experience of life. William of Tocco rightly observes that the portentousness of his memory, the beautiful leaps of his imagination, his gift for making intuitive connections, and the exuberant richness of his intimate life, which we admire especially in his liturgical poetry, were all due to this "most tender constitution." This spiritual refinement and sensibility put him in the company of such privileged souls as Francis of Assisi, Raphael, Mozart, and Goethe, along with the powerful spirits of Eckehart, Dante, Michelangelo, Beethoven (Stakemeier).

The refined makeup of his soul was accompanied by a virile courage that was free of sentimentality or personal vanity, and a coolly resolute power of decision, which manifested itself particularly in the face of danger. Such was the case when the ship taking him to Paris was threatened by a furious storm with an imminent danger of complete shipwreck, in which he alone was able to retain a composure so calm as to inspire courage in the other people onboard until they were out of danger. Neither his mother's prayers, nor his sisters' tears, nor his brothers' brutality, nor even long months of captivity in his father's castle were able to shake the steely will with which he had freely chosen the ideal of his new Order. Yet, despite this firmness, Thomas never offended or harmed anyone either by word or in deed. It is true that, against his adversaries in Paris, in order to defend the truth, he knew how to express his thoughts with resoluteness, but his righteous indignation—both verbal and written—never exceeded its just measure. Because of nobility of spirit and awareness of an innate strength, rather than out of weakness, he showed himself meek and understanding toward the rejections and errors of his environment. Thomas possessed what Italians call "gentilezza" [gentility]: that refined and chivalrous manner, ever responsive to need and full of attentions, which issues from profound self-possession and trust in the good. In addition to this gentility, he possessed "dulcedo" [sweetness], radiant amiability and goodness, and the aristocratic delicacy of Francis of Assisi, Catherine of Siena, Philip Neri, and John Bosco. His contemporaries called him "the kindly and beloved master," and even Eckehart speaks with emotion of the "dear St. Thomas."

The famous theologian and man of science showed sincere respect for the little and the weak who are frequently so great and so strong in the eyes of God. He wrote that a little old woman full of faith understands much more concerning the divine things than a proud, learned man without faith who knows how to weave magisterial syllogisms on the First Principle of things (*In Symbolum Apostolorum expositio*, prologue).

* * *

The spiritual development of St. Thomas does not display the same sudden leaps and gaps as that of a St. Augustine. From the very beginning, his happy constitution exhibited the mark of a psychological-physical unity. During his childhood, he grew like a strong, tender shoot in the garden of the Church without ever having to succumb to the terrible struggle between the senses and the spirit. The harmony that reigned within him could be troubled only with difficulty. Trustworthy witnesses, such as Br. Reginald, his confessor, attest that he never felt or willingly allowed any temptations of the flesh. Being well regulated in all things, he knew how to arrange his day in a beautiful order: early in the morning, he celebrated the Holy Sacrifice; then he served the Mass of one of his brethren; finally, he mounted the pulpit to preach or took the professor's chair to teach his lesson. He showed no preference regarding different foods at table and immersed himself in his queries with such intensity that he never even noticed whether or not he had been served. During the hours set aside for recreation, he could be seen striding with resolute steps through the garden or the cloister, always in meditation, yet always ready to respond affably to the brothers who stopped to speak with him. His afternoons were spent either writing or dictating; and he abandoned himself to contemplation of divine things from after the evening meal until late into the night.

Where he was strict with himself, he was humane and reasonable with others. He allowed them the small and innocent joys of life, and taught expressly that humor and amusements have their place in helping us to bear our daily sufferings, which are far from few. In so doing, he succinctly unmasked the deep hypocrisy of a puritanical pharisaism.

* * *

In full freedom, he chose for himself the flower of the most sublime donation to God in a life of virginity. The breath of his purity communicated itself more and more to his whole person, revealing the admirable impartiality and sureness of a man who has never experienced within himself the rupture caused by grave fault. His radiant purity was not, however, insensitivity; indeed, in the latter, he saw a distortion and defect of the soul that goes straight against the order of nature (ST II-II, q. 142, a. 1). The true foundation of a life of virginity is not the devaluation of the sensitive, a Neoplatonic reduction, or Stoic denial. He warned emphatically against a false rigorism that would consider normal conjugal life as something inferior and unsuitable. For him, as for the Apostle, a life of virginity is only for those who wish to serve God without obstacles and who wish to dedicate themselves to contemplation with a fuller and more pure freedom (ST II-II, q. 152, a. 1, ad 1).

It is in this total dedication to God that Thomas perceived his life's ideal and from it that his life drew its enchantment and its beauty. His was a spirit fixed unwaveringly on God. It is not without reason that painters of old have emphasized this trait of his personality. Theology was for him "sacred doctrine," holy and sanctifying, which lifts us above all natural perspectives and, with grace, is a participation in the intimate life of the Three Divine Persons. For this reason, St. Thomas adamantly insisted that chastity and interior purity of will are necessary for the knowledge of God. From impurity, he says, is born the blindness of a mind no longer open to the truth of divine things and then the paralysis of a soul unable to operate for its own salvation, foolishness, apathetic sloth, and hardness of heart (ST II-II, q. 56, a. 3).[a] With keen psychological observation, he shows that perfect dedication to the Divine Goodness gradually lessens the force of the lower inclinations, directing all the limited energies of our being toward the Supreme Good.

* * *

Thus, for St. Thomas, sublime thoughts stand in a peace that is outside time, beyond all subjectivity and personal situations. It is truth in itself speaking here, the word of God in its inexhaustible fullness, and the theologian watches over it with respectful tranquility. Because St. Thomas's temperament was both that of mystic and researcher, his symbol is the radiant sun that, like a ruby, shines from his breast. The brightest clarity of thought and an impassioned mystical experience grew within him in a deep organic unity, joined together to form a single trait of his nature.

Although it is true that the first step toward God occurs through Faith, Faith can apprehend the divine only analogically, under the veil of human concepts. Love, on the other hand, transports us into God insofar as it unites us directly to him, attaining to him in a manner far more perfect than Faith. Love transforms us into new creatures, impressing upon the soul a growing likeness to the divine nature, and thus it communicates to us the foundations for a new and more profound understanding of the Divinity.

St. Thomas saw the effect of the gift of wisdom that the Holy Spirit infuses in us together with love in this experience of the divine. As love's most delicate flower, this wisdom grows and brings us to a sort of accord with and an affinity for the Deity, a "connaturality" with the Divinity. It renders us apt to live the sacred, to experience something of its mysteries beyond all our conceptions, to touch its inner reign, to taste its secret happiness.

---

[a] Rather, ST II-II, q. 15, a. 3.

God alone was ever the end of all of Thomas Aquinas's longing. Even as an adolescent in the monastery of Montecassino, he often asked his teachers, "Who is God?" All throughout his life, he did nothing more than to reflect upon that answer, and his yearning to attain the vision of God without veils became a burning flame by which, when not yet fifty, he was consumed.

Conversations on St. John of God

Just what resonance these *Gespräche um Johannes von Gott* by Ludwig Ruland will be able to have, I do not know. I sincerely hope that the approach taken by the author will meet with an understanding adequate to foster imitators who will have the same deep appreciation that he has of human things as well as his respect for things divine. Published in 1947, this little book is the labor of the Catholic publisher Ferdinand Schöningh of Würzburg, and is one of the first fraternal greetings to come to us from Germany in this post-war era. This greeting, which has as ambassador the saint of mercy, develops page by page, from beginning to end, the theme of using one's own immolation to relieve the suffering of others, to eradicate injustices, and to fertilize the little corner of goodness that every human heart retains of its divine origin. For each Christian, but especially for the saints, life has its starting point in the condemnation of this world. Even before Christianity, Socrates himself glimpsed this when he said to the judges that "it is better to suffer than to do injustice" (*Apol.* 32 bd).[a] The point of arrival, or better yet, the sphere of action of such a life is the infinite expanse of the works of mercy. The true point of arrival is the love that the saint bears for God, which is also the true starting point from the Christian perspective, rather than the merely human love of Socrates. In this sense, the works of mercy can be called an exteriorization of that interior love of the creature for its Creator, because the dialogue of the saints with creatures is no more than the echo of their dialogue with God, its fruit, and its testimony. The intimate relationship of the saint with God is tied to a secret. Since the way of sanctity is precisely the opposite of that of curiosity, this secret is hidden from every profane gaze. Each saint has

---

[a] Cf. Plato, *Apology* 32b–d.

possessed his secret, which has bound him to God in the abandonment of complete immolation. Since we, imprisoned as we are by our few half-baked ideas, are in the dark concerning that secret, whatever appears to us as incoherent or even repulsive is in fact what links and explains these harmonies, which the Holy Spirit educes from our fragile human nature when the latter listens with docility to that same Spirit's ineffable invitations.

This little book is an attempt to fathom such a secret through a deepened knowledge of the fragility of the flesh. This is a bold undertaking, which though carried out in the feeble glow of an indirect light, attempts to respond to that question most compelling to our curiosity: Are the saints like or unlike us? Christian common sense answers that they were like us, but that they lived differently than us, that is, they possessed all our passions of body and soul, but they bore the first generously and struggled with the second without yielding. This little book takes a step forward in showing that some of the saints at least suffered bodily passions more painful and more deeply discordant than our own. Yet, they were able to "transfigure" them into the heavenly joyousness of the cardinal and theological virtues and of the gifts of the Holy Spirit with a will that was indomitable and docile to divine grace.

The new method, presented in recent years and in different measures by other authors of hagiographical studies, attacks the facile hagiographical tradition, which portrays Christ's most faithful imitators as though they were exempt from our misery, perpetually surrounded by a halo of glory even during the course of their earthly lives. Positivism attempted to demonstrate that the halo in question was one of smoke, and sanctity and mysticism no more than abnormalities in the functioning of our vital activities, phenomena indicative of evasion, if not always of degeneration, as some researchers were willing to argue. The respectful recognition granted to Christian mysticism in Henri Bergson's last work, *The Two Sources of Morality and Religion*,[b] has dealt justly with such profanations and made it possible for the Christian hagiographer to explore the life of the spirit according to his own proper criterion. Yet, the present little book admonishes that none of those things which can befall our poor human nature are, in themselves, opposed to grace, neither the illnesses and physical flaws, which like us, the saints may have had, nor even spiritual flaws themselves, excluding, of course, any attachment

---

[b] *Les deux sources de la morale et de la religion.*

to evil. This method then is an arduous one which finds itself in its earliest applications and which ought to be followed with thoughtful attention. The study of man, the metaphysics of the spirit, so to speak, by merit of new currents of thought, has entered into a phase, which reveals not a few points of contact with the most authentic Christian tradition. It pertains to "spiritual theology" to ensure that its method does not cross its boundaries or trespass onto forbidden ground.

Ludwig Ruland, having held the chairs of moral theology, pastoral theology, homiletics, and Christian sociology in the University of Würzburg from 1913 to 1938 (according to the information provided by a note appended to the volume), is a veteran of university teaching. He has ably entrusted the development of his analysis to that most cordial form of exploration of the truth, which is the dialogue. This form breaks away from all continuity of discourse that is external and systematic, in favor of an approach that is more interior, one that constitutes the interlocutors' secret center of convergence. These interlocutors are the prior, the physician, and the professor. The first of these, the prior, basing himself on the first "Life" of St. John of God, written in 1580 by Francisco Castro, summarizes the biography of the saint in austere passages shorn of all rhetorical baggage. These passages are subsequently offered to the other two interlocutors, each of whom seeks to place those facts back within their real, original framework—according to the point of view of his own field of study—through the interrogation of medicine and history. In the course of this peaceful search for the subjective and objective conditions of the saint's existence, of the "situation," as they say today, distrust is cast upon the "Life" written in 1623 by Bishop Govea, which like that of Castro was also received by the Bollandists. Yet, aside from a congeries of visions, miracles, and supernatural manifestations, which lack any critical foundation and are due exclusively to the baroque imagination of its author, it adds nothing to the latter and principal source. It is to be lamented that later historians, unfortunately, have drawn more on Govea than on Castro.

Using Castro's narrative, the two experts of the "Dialogue" seek to retrace the subjective and objective conditions mentioned earlier which Castro, bound as he was by the cultural perspective of his own time and lacking both a historical sense and psychological sensitivity, did not feel the need to examine. Thus the professor, with broad and effective expositions, introduces us to seventeenth-century Spanish life by describing the various social classes and clarifying the distances and clashes between them. He also shows the enormous force that faith exercised both on the suffering and those rejected by fortune in bearing their unspeakable miseries, as well as its influence on those few favored ones who knew how to respond and frequently did so at the request of the saint, with a generosity equal to the faith that they professed. This explains the access that the saint had to the doors of the powerful, even of the king himself, and therefore the inexhaustibility of his means of assistance.

Much more arduous has been the task of the physician, which constitutes the truly original aspect of the volume. As is known, the biography of St. John of God portrays patterns and circumstances that are altogether unique. He ran away from home at the age of eight; among other things, this led even to the loss of his family name. It is for this reason that his new hosts called him John of God, according to the custom of the times. This suggests to the physician the hypothesis that John may have inherited a schizophrenic condition that disposed him to intermittent fits of "motor restlessness" and may have driven him to take up a new type of life abruptly. A vigorous youth, he attempted a career at arms, but suffered a grievous head wound in a fall from his horse, from which he was healed only after great sufferings. However, as the physician informs us, the healing from the physical trauma did not comport in itself a similar healing of the wounds that may have occurred in the deeper areas of the psyche, especially if we take into account a congenital schizophrenic condition. Then (and we note this as a simple hypothesis for consideration), in light of the most characteristic feature of the saint's biography, namely, his admittance to the insane asylum at Granada, the physician asserts that this may well have been an episode of real insanity and not, as has been believed until now, of insanity simulated for ascetical reasons. To this type of disorder, the physician also attributes the urge for sudden changes in direction observable in the life of the saint, as well as the difficulty he experienced in recollecting himself in prayer. However, this perspective must not be misunderstood. It does not wish, in any way, to eliminate or to lessen the supernatural reality of this exceptional life in which the very gravity of the "disease" allows the untamed energy of John's spirit and the work of divine grace to emerge more clearly. He directs the operation of a great hospital down to the least detail, supports several works of charity at the same time, being present everywhere with sound common sense regarding the realities of life. When the occasion warrants, he makes use of the most sophisticated methods of human and Christian prudence for the good of those subject to him.

According to the physician, the case of St. John of God may not be the only instance in which an individual with an abnormal physico-psychic constitution reached sanctity. He cites the work of Fischer[c] on St. Camillus de Lellis,[d] who may have had a schitzothymic condition. This might help to explain the conflict between St. Camillus and St. Philip Neri, his confessor, as well as the fits of temper into which, despite his best intentions, he fell with his associates. Amid the emotion and to the edification of those present, he would then shed tears of bitter repentance. God, it seems, wished to try these two saints of mercy, both of whom experienced the most repugnant sufferings of body and spirit, with similar afflictions in order that their detachment from self and their dedication to their brethren might know no bounds. Far from denying the supernatural, the physician actually intends to underline its efficacy and eminence. Moreover, he attributes to it the incident when the saint heroically rescued all the hospitalized patients from a fire without suffering any harm to himself—a miracle mentioned in both the Bull of canonization and in the prayer for his feast. Although his own interpretation leans toward the hypothesis of a "psychic trauma" caused by wounds to the meninges and cortex, he does not rule out Malvy's explanation, which attributes the episode of insanity to the interior crisis or emotional "shock"[e] caused by the intensity of his repentance for his own sins. However, considering the complexity of hereditary and natural factors, which occur even in those consciences that pass for normal, perhaps the two explanations are not irreconcilable.

Yet in the life of man, even the gravest and most painful misfortunes serve the inscrutable designs of Providence, especially where there is docile submission to the motions of God. The physician is the one who points out that, for John, forced rest among the mentally ill, the barbarous treatment then used on those unfortunates notwithstanding, produced his return to a normal form of life. "With the passing of years, the interior impulse toward change and action can no longer be satisfied by the exterior necessities of the desired ideal. To rent or purchase houses to welcome the sick and the poor, and to seek alms ceaselessly for their support, corresponded to the deepest inclination of his nature. Under the

---

[c] "Foscher" in *Profili di Santi*.
[d] Cf. Michael Fischer, *Der heilige Kamillus von Lellis* (Freiburg: Caritasverlag, 1940).
[e] Cf. Antoine Malvy, "Saint Jean de Dieu a-t-il simulé la folie?," *Études* 191 (May 1927): 427–438.

unceasing illumination and guidance of His grace, the soul that gives itself wholly to God then builds a sanctity of rare greatness upon the foundation of such a nature."[f]

This sober declaration which can serve as a commentary to the "*Virtus in infirmitate perficitur*" [power is made perfect in weakness][g] of St. Paul, sums up the new criterion followed by the author. At issue, then, is that "thorn" that God often fixes in the flesh of saints and of the greater spirits so that it may be for them both a continuous "reminder" of their natural misery and the bond by which He keeps them tied to Himself in ineffable love. Dr. Ruland does not say this, but it can be read between the lines.

To the modern scholars of the *gesta sanctorum* [deeds of the saints], which are so rich in both divine and human sense, we entrust the new method, so that they may recover the authentic face of our saints, steeped in suffering and transfigured by divine grace.

---

[f] Ludwig Ruland, *Gespräche um Johannes von Gott* (Würzburg: Verlag Ferdinand Schöningh, 1947), 116–117.

[g] 2 Cor 12:9.

Edith Stein

FROM PHILOSOPHY TO MARTYRDOM

There is no doubt regarding the sad end of this eminent thinker, formerly assistant to Husserl; however, not yet known to us are the final details in this additional cruelty by the idolatry of "blood" against the natural equality of human beings and their divine fraternity in Christ. The memories and testimonies of all who had contact with her during the various stages of her life—the years of strict discipline in her Jewish family, her years of undergraduate studies at the University, the first years of her conversion, her religious life, and during the stops on her last voyage toward martyrdom—have been gathered with loving care by the Cologne Carmel of "Mary of Peace" where she was welcomed as a postulant in 1933 and where she made her religious profession in 1935. This bright crown of white and crimson flowers was interwoven by the present prioress, Renata of the Holy Spirit (*Edith Stein, Lebensbild einer Philosophin und Karmeliten*, Bei Glock und Lutz in Nuremberg, 1948).[a] As the assistant Mistress of Novices to our Sr. Teresa Benedicta of the Cross,[b] she was better able than anyone to garner the inner traits of this soul who burned with a thirst for truth, who had offered herself as a sacrifice to God in order to turn aside his wrath from his people.

The earthly journey of Edith Stein represents the complete development of the single, profound, and radical aspiration by which her soul was seized while she was yet a girl. By an inscrutable impulse, this aspiration worked external circumstances into stimuli to an ever more intimate approach to truth. Stein never practiced the religion of her

---

[a] English trans. from Teresia Renata Posselt, *Edith Stein: The Life of a Philosopher and Carmelite* (Washington, DC: ICS Publications, 2005).
[b] All references indicate that Posselt was actually Mistress of Novices and not the assistant.

forebears during her youth in her hometown of Breslau, though as the last and most beloved daughter of her venerable mother, she willingly accompanied her to the synagogue out of filial duty. The first stage, then, was atheism, understood as the absence of the religious problem. Her first strong impression of the Absolute came at Göttingen, from philosophy, at the school of Edmund Husserl, the founder of phenomenology. The significant number of conversions within the circle that gravitated around Husserl at the University is suggestive. Leaving aside Max Scheler, the vicissitudes of whose profound and restless spirit are well known, one mentions notably, Adolf Reinach, who converted along with his wife and daughter and who died as a war hero in 1917; Siegfried Hamburger, who embraced the religious life; and Dietrich von Hildebrand, who enrolled in the Third Order of St. Francis of Assisi. Baptized later were Alexandre Koyré, together with his wife, as well as Erika Gothe. This "appeal" of God also resounded in Stein as the climax of the integral search for truth that she had heard announced by her teacher, who was unable to exhaust the essences that he studied despite his penetrating skills as their investigator. It is to Husserl's exacting method that we owe the gradual way in which this virginal soul came to an awareness of the problem of God: free from any sudden, dramatic turns of events, but free also from any infidelity, drawn as if by ever-increasing rays from a constant stream of light that became more brilliant at each stage. Along with this awareness, came faithfulness to that interior revelation, a fidelity which lead Stein to unconditional acceptance of the cross regarding which she had had premonitions since her earliest steps in the faith. Upon Edith's announcement to her grief-stricken mother: "Mother, I am a Catholic,"[c] for the first time, that noble woman, who had borne the burden of educating her seven children alone, burst into tears; and mother and daughter shed tears together in a mutual and inexpressible sorrow.

Like all deep souls, Edith was taken with the intimate language of the Catholic liturgy. Every year, until her entry into Carmel, she went to Beuron for the liturgy of Holy Week. Dom Raphael Walzer, the Archabbot of Beuron, was her first spiritual father. As a soul strongly inclined to the speculative, she fell under the allure of St. Thomas Aquinas, whom she studied in depth. With sure intuition, she drew out his perennial values from her study and boldly inserted them within the framework of Husserlian thought. The presentations she made at several cultural meetings provide excellent evidence of her scientific activity.

---

[c] Posselt, *Edith Stein*, 348, ch. 7, T 1.

She made a profound impression on Archbishop Waitz at Salzburg, and in 1937, during a meeting dedicated to the study of phenomenology, in Juvisy near Paris, she took the reins of the discussion with a competence and modesty that generated general enthusiasm. Her predilection for the Angelic Doctor turned especially toward the problem of knowledge. She dedicated a perceptive article to it in the celebratory volume that the disciples of Husserl presented to him for his seventieth birthday (1929). Her translation of the difficult text of *De veritate* into German astonished specialists with its insight into the text's most recondite notions and for the apt agreement of the Thomistic terms with the phenomenological school.

Aware of the exceptional gift that Providence had made to Carmel, she was required by her superiors after she had become a religious to continue her scholarly research. The fruits of this second period of scientific activity are her essays on pure metaphysics as well as her original analysis of the mystical doctrine of St. John of the Cross. Her scholastic activity was varied and it received full public acknowledgement in 1932 with her appointment to teach in the German Institute for Scientific Pedagogy in Münster. A mere year later (she gave her last lesson on February 25, 1933) she was torn away from this position by the drastic anti-Semitic measures of the Nazi government.

By then, Edith had already progressed greatly in her self-gift to God. The boarding students who were with her at the Marianum in Münster remember her as an image of sweetness and fortitude, who bravely endured every sort of privation, even of the most basic conveniences. Being gentle and quick to help everyone, even with regard to small, innocent pleasures, she once provided her students with fruit for an outing when they were short on cash, and one time she gave the blanket off her bed to a poor man who had nothing with which to cover himself. Being possessed of a temperament that was both delicate and resilient, she quickly became aware of the afflictions suffered by others and knew how to discern the right way to offer comfort and charity. Therefore, in reading the testimonies of the boarders, the moving certainty that "Fraulein Dr. Stein" was truly a saint, a soul wholly God's, comes as no surprise. Both they and the Dominican superior at Cologne, who numbered her among her instructors, witnessed that their eminent teacher studied and prayed in her little chamber until late at night and yet was the first to reach the chapel in the morning, even before the sisters, remaining there motionless and recollected at her kneeler for as many as three Masses.

Her sisters in religion remember her for her simplicity and humility. Upon entering the cloister, her self-effacement was so great that almost no one was aware of her higher formation or of the quality of her exceptional intelligence. Though she was still very involved in her own studies and in the convent's internal school, she was eager for the most humble offices, including those in the kitchen. However, her results there were somewhat mediocre. She fought a ceaseless war against her ego, resulting in the blossoming of the most resplendent flowers of charity and humility. The pained dismay which froze the communities at Cologne and at Echt in Holland, at having her torn from the nests into which she had been received as a refugee, gives witness to the attraction which Edith exercised by her total dedication. Conscious of the terrible storm threatening her people from the first rise of Hitler to power, she offered herself as victim for their salvation and conversion to Christ. She had the joy of having Rose, her elder sister, close to her—first in the religious life (as a Carmelite tertiary) and later in her torment. Her passion for the cross is made plain in her explanation of the Carmelite vocation: "It is not human activity that can help us but the Passion of Christ. It is a share in that, that I desire."[d]

Carmelite life infused into her a peace of spirit, a fullness of life, and an ineffable joy of heart that radiated to those who, on rare occasions, were able to approach her. There was in her open and youthful appearance an evident dignity of simplicity a charitable affability, a fraternal understanding from which emanates the striking sense of mingled joy and pain felt whenever we are touched in this wretched existence of ours by some authentic ray of the Infinite Goodness. The Archabbot of Beuron, who was one of its earliest witnesses, wrote that "I have seldom met a soul that united so many excellent qualities; she was simplicity and naturalness personified. She was completely a woman, gentle and even maternal, without ever wanting to 'mother' anyone. Gifted with mystical graces, in the true sense of the word, she never gave any sign of affectation or a sense of superiority. She was simple with simple people, learned with the learned yet without presumption, an inquirer with inquirers, and I would almost like to add, a sinner with sinners."[e] The few fragments of her spiritual writings and correspondence, which were saved, by chance, from destruction in an

---

[d] Posselt, *Edith Stein*, 262n20.
[e] Posselt, *Edith Stein*, 80.

ill-advised fearful attempt to avoid reprisals, afford a glimpse into the richness of this soul's supernatural life, a soul who, like Teresa of Avila, asked only to suffer or die.

She obtained both. In the summer of 1942, the SS went to remove her, along with her sister Rose, from the convent that had been hosting her, where owing to the direct intervention of the President of the Swiss Confederation, Dr. Egger, they had been waiting, moment to moment, for police permission to go to the Carmel of Le Pâquier in Switzerland. From there her agony proceeded: first, in the camp near Amersfoort in Northern Holland, then through Germany, and finally to Auschwitz in Poland, where they must have undergone unspeakable privations and maltreatments, from which they were freed by a kindly death, probably in the gas chamber. In a note to the Mother Superior, Sr. Benedicta writes: "A *scientia crucis* [knowledge of the Cross] can be gained only when one comes to feel the Cross radically. I have been convinced of that from the first moment and have said, from my heart: *Ave, Crux, spes unica!* [Hail, Cross, our only hope!]"[f]

It is with stones such as these, bright with their own blood, that the City of God is illuminated.

---

[f] English trans. from Edith Stein to Mother Ambrosia Antonia Engelmann, presumably December, 1941, in *Self-Portrait in Letters, 1916–1942*, trans. Josephine Koeppel (Washington, DC: ICS Publications, 1993), 341, no. 330.

Bartolomea Capitanio

THE LITTLE TEACHER OF LOVERE

The new interest in the lives of the saints, especially of those closer to our time, felt for some time now, prefers to turn more directly to their writings, to the authentic itinerary of their intimate martyrdom, without amplification. Although she died young, Capitanio has left us three large volumes of writings; of greatest interest, particularly for our purpose, is the first, containing her letters to the most varied addressees. For me, it is a delightful collection of letters, not only for its content, but also for its form, which suggests a creature bold yet timid, exuberant yet recollected, active yet contemplative, who was capable not only of being interested in the humblest tasks and the most fragile things, but also of soaring aloft in exploration of the most hidden secrets of the human heart and the most difficult problems of Divine Providence.

What is more, Capitanio did this unexpectedly, as if by intuition, without being doctrinaire or using trite clichés, drawing instead from her interior and turning with docility to the Divine Spouse. Indeed, our saint stands alone on the path of sanctity and is not bound to any specific type of spirituality. It is true that in her childhood she was educated by the Poor Clares; however, she did not wish to remain there, despite the urging of the good sisters, who had well understood the worth of their exceptional student. Her first spiritual director, Don Angelo Bosio, a priest wholly given to the labors of ministry, directed his penitent in the practical foundation of the Christian virtues and of the most urgent forms of the apostolate.

The exceptionally supernatural seems to be almost absent from her writings, with only vague hints of aspirations, presentiments, secret ardors, surges of zeal. Like St. Catherine of Siena, the little teacher of Lovere was in a hurry. She knew that her life would soon end and she wished to work to accomplish the task that had begun to burn in her heart when she was only an adolescent: to save the souls of those most in need and most abandoned, the souls of children, young girls, the sick, the elderly. There she is, at the center of a circle of pious associations—most notably the Disciples of the Lord, formed by twelve priests and seventy-two virgins, and the Compagnia di S. Luigi [Company of St. Aloysius Gonzaga] for young girls—in which Capitanio began to carry out a program of apostolate that makes her a genial forerunner of Catholic Action.

Her collected letters are the echo of her activity. Well might it be called the letter collection of haste and friendship: mostly brief notes, replies, requests, errands, in which one finds a confidence or passing thought, without superfluities, such as occur (as she herself confirmed) after a hard day of work, late at night, when sleep weighs down the eyelids. Yet suddenly the eagle takes flight, at which point it is necessary to follow her toward the sun. With the attitude of a true spiritual teacher, the youth of barely seventeen wrote to her friend Marianna Vertova, "But now let us come to the point," and traced a whole plan of life, exhortations, counsels. The letter cited, which is among her earliest, already contains her whole method of spiritual friendship; then the saint herself became aware of having betrayed herself somewhat: "You will say that I want to act the spiritual teacher, while I am not even good enough to act the student. You are right, and this is an effect of my overly refined pride, which would like only to teach and not to be taught" (*Lett.* 3).[a] However, she wished her friend to understand that her heart is always open, "If your letters were to be one hundred thousand pages long, I would certainly not tire of reading them. I want to believe that you will be the same way. Oh! Alright, farewell, because I seem unable to be done" (Ibid.: I follow the numbering provided in vol. I of *Scritti spirituali*, Modena 1904).

* * *

What is immediately striking in her letters is a friendship that grows by a surge of affection, her concise and direct way of expressing herself, with a sincerity that is substantiated by what she says. She was incapable

---

[a] Bartolomea Capitanio to Marianna Vertova, August 21, 1824, in *Scritti spirituali*, vol. 1 (Modena: Tipografia Pontificia ed Arcivescovile dell'Immacolata Concezione, 1904), Letter 3.

of magnifying artificial emotions, powerless to supress those that touched her heart, whether trust or discouragement, heavenly ravishment or inconsolable anguish.

After the death of her father, whom she had led back to the practice of religion, she went to a priest for a suffrage Mass and apologized for not having first thanked him for his presence at the funeral, "We have not called on you before now to do our duty because, as sorrow for our loss is at its greatest, every little reminder has made it unbearable for us" (*Lett.* 21).[b]

This crushing sorrow continued to increase since, three days later, the mourning daughter wrote to Don Angelo Taeri of Brescia: "As you will know, the Lord has deprived me of the dearest thing that I had in this world; this loss is being felt most sharply by my heart, so that I cannot find peace. Pray to God for me and say a 'Requiem' for the soul of the one whom God has stolen from me that he may grant rest to him and calmness to me" (*Lett.* 227).[c] That same day (November 30, 1831), she requested a consoling visit from the sister of that same priest: "Console me sometime by visiting me; this will give me great pleasure and will do much to lift up my afflicted heart" (*Lett.* 22).[d] It was the deepest desolation yet for this spirit nearly at the pinnacle of detachment, who would shortly leave her mother and sister to found her Institute (1832); she will then say promptly that "God is master of all," while "tears and affliction stifle every word in me" (*Lett.* 249).[e]

Her filial love was matched by her friendship. Capitanio's friendship was so immense, so generous, so ardent, so eager for understanding and reciprocation, so solicitous and vital, that we must say that she transfused her life and the highest tension of her spirit in it. With the members of the Company of the Disciples of the Lord, her tone was tailored to the personality and needs of each one. However, her favorite, the friend of her heart, who must surely have been worthy of her holy friend, was Lucia Sigismondi (Cismondi). Poured out in these almost seventy letters is an exchange so transparent, a communication so ardent and so full of all the mysteries, yearnings, joys, and uncertainties of love, as to see love almost realized in its purest essence.

---

[b] Capitanio to Bortolo Celeri, November 16, 1831, in *Scritti spirituali*, Letter 224.
[c] Capitanio to Angelo Taeri, November 30, 1831, in *Scritti spirituali*, Letter 227.
[d] Capitanio to Regina Taeri, November 30, 1831, in *Scritti spirituali*, Letter 228.
[e] Capitanio to her sister, November 16, 1832, in *Scritti spirituali*, Letter 249.

The most affectionate designations and expressions bloom when Capitanio writes to Cismondi. There is a quick shift from the "most distinguished lady" of the first letter,[f] to "sweetest one, dearest friend and sister, more than dearest, my most darling, most delightful, and most amiable one, your Cia."[g] In an outburst of sincerity, she confessed to her, "Believe that you are truly engraved in my heart and in my mind; no day goes by and almost no hour, on which my Lucia does not come to my mind" (*Lett.* 66).[h] At other times, she writes that her friend's letters "console more than anything in this world" (*Lett.* 75);[i] that "conversing and speaking with you, sweet sister, it seems to me that my heart is overcome with joy, and a sweet consolation infuses all of me. What then, will be the case, if it should be my beautiful lot to enjoy you in Paradise?" (*Lett.* 87).[j] She stated that she wished that they could die together, rise together, and "go together to see Jesus and Mary in Paradise for the first time" (*Lett.* 82).[k] To her confessor, she described her friend as a saint: "Just now, I read a letter from the dearest of my friends, who is truly a saint, Lucia Cismondi."[l] In addition, she wrote to the friend herself an account of an aspiration received during Communion rejoicing that, "I cannot keep to myself that I seem to know that the Lord is very happy with you; that you are very dear to him. Since I asked him to tell me if he desired something of you, I seem to understand that the Lord has destined you to be among the greatest of the saints and that what he requires of you is a particular conformity to his graces in order that you may make yourself a great saint" (*Lett.* 121).[m] Moreover, Cismondi was the one who foretold Capitanio's approaching death (*Lett.* 163).[n]

Of a different nature, but with the same rhythm and ardor, are her letters to her confessor. These are similar in tone to those of St. Catherine of Siena, St. Teresa of Avila, St. Margaret Mary Alacoque, and St. Gemma Galgani. In her case, as in that of these saints, the humble penitent, by

---

[f] "Pregiatissima Signora" (Capitanio to Lucia Cismondi, July 23, 1826, in *Scritti spirituali*, Letter 40).

[g] "Dolcissima, carissima amica e sorella, la più che carissima, l'arcicarissima, la dilettissima, l'amabilissima, la sua Cia."

[h] Capitanio to Cismondi, July 19, 1827, in *Scritti spirituali*, Letter 66.

[i] Capitanio to Cismondi, December 4, 1827, in *Scritti spirituali*, Letter 85.

[j] Capitanio to Cismondi, February 2, 1829, in *Scritti spirituali*, Letter 137.

[k] Capitanio to Cismondi, November 9, 1827, in *Scritti spirituali*, Letter 82.

[l] Capitanio to Angelo Bosio, August 28, 1827, in *Scritti spirituali*, Letter 71.

[m] Capitanio to Cismondi, November 3, 1828, in *Scritti spirituali*, Letter 121.

[n] Capitanio to Cismondi, June 15, 1829, in *Scritti spirituali*, Letter 163.

the mysterious effect of a spiritual "exchange," becomes both guide and teacher to her guide. Later, when Don Angelo became seriously ill due to excessive work, his spiritual daughter organized a veritable crusade of prayers, consoled him with her notes, and even managed to slip into his room where she almost fainted in reaction to the miserable conditions in which she found him. However, she also rejoiced in having been the one to encourage him on the way of the cross. The tone and content of this invitation dated June 1, 1827, are entirely confounding in that they come from a youth:

> Now, I am joyful and happy but I hope that Mary and, even more, the Holy Spirit will also console Your Reverence. I was too afflicted hearing of your suffering. . . . Allow me to tell you my feeling in this regard, even though it is not a thing pertaining to me.
>
> To tell you the truth, all along I was wondering to myself and could not understand why the Lord, who usually repays those souls who labor for his glory with crosses, did not allow to Your Reverence anything but honors and praise. I have prayed that the Lord would arrange it so that you become the person most humbled, contradicted, abandoned, injured, etc. However, the Lord willed to resolve my perplexity by allowing your suffering to become known to me. May he be thanked for it. As much as it pains me to see you so afflicted, I am equally consoled, and last night, for this matter, I recited the "Te Deum," twice thanking the Lord for deigning to enrich your soul with great graces. (*Lett.* 64)°

Perhaps the frankest manifestation of her personality is found in the protest she sent to her confessor when he was named Rector of the Seminary of Brescia (a nomination that never went through). She, along with the whole population of Lovere and its aged provost, whose principal support Don Bosio was, were oppressed by the thought of losing him. Her letter is dated March 7, 1832, when she was on the point of bringing her foundation to birth. The theme of the letter is "Glory to Jesus and His Most Holy Cross!"

> Most Reverend Father Confessor,
> I do not know how to begin this letter of mine. I would like to silence my self-love and to let Jesus, whom I have invoked fervently, speak.

° Capitanio to Bosio, June 1, 1827, in *Scritti spirituali*, Letter 64.

> With the greatest regret, first I heard, and then read in your own very fine letter, of the very strange enterprise that you had taken upon yourself. Such a great misfortune for our town! . . . But I must acknowledge that I have deserved this.
>
> Just now, I saw our Most Reverend Provost [and here she describes the anguish of that venerable priest] . . .
>
> He said a great many other things that I do not wish to repeat to you, but they could move even stones to tenderness. I cannot understand how Your Reverence can have accepted such an office since you are aware of the very critical circumstances of our town, for which God seems to have made you exactly to be of service. . . . Is it perhaps charity to do ill to one in order to be of service to another? . . .
>
> As for our project and the Lord's work, believe that it will surely be dashed to the ground because no one wants to take on the risk of such a great work without support, and were one to proceed without it, it would only deceive. I say no more, I fully deserve this, and I have already made a sacrifice of it. However, God is good and we will have so many prayers made to him that he will yield. Listen to him, and consider that it was not a coincidence that you were born in Lovere . . .
>
> May God speak to your heart and have you understand his will.[p]

The end of the letter expresses her complete desolation: "I, too, find myself in a fine predicament, without health, without the possibility of becoming a nun (if I had done so when it was timely, I should now be there), bereft of any hope of doing what I so much desire to do. My God, I beg you, help me" (*Lett.* 230). However, just a week later, on March 14, the humble disciple goes back and tramples her own suffering underfoot, a suffering which at first had been so impetuous and so prophetic, retracting not her thoughts, which remain unchanged, but rather her fierce insistence (*Lett.* 231).

Her sanctity, if it is proper to put it this way, was a "sanctity of obstinacy." From the moment when, as a young pupil with the Poor Clares, she drew the long straw destining her to sanctity, she accepted her lot with dismay and tears, but also with resolve. That will, catching fire at the dawn of her life, revealed to her who she was. Certainly, she was conscious of her abilities and of what was maturing with unshakable

---

[p] Capitanio to Bosio, March 7, 1832, in *Scritti spirituali*, Letter 230.

certitude within her soul. She was not so blind as to be unaware of how she was esteemed nor could she fail to perceive the position that she held in the center of her small world. It was this acute awareness that others considered an indication of her undisputed superiority, which unleashed upon her life a tempest designed to afflict her life with frightening shocks. All the energy of her implacable will was turned toward this point, fixed on this ever-open wound. The records of her examinations of conscience (which are still preserved) detail the martyrdom of a will simultaneously so severe and faithful to itself. They form quite possibly a unique document in Christian hagiography.

The description that Capitanio gives of her pride is worthy of a treatise on the deepest humility. Here is how she lays herself open to Cismondi:

> Believe me, dear Lucia, I speak to you with all the sincerity of my heart. This passion is so rooted in me that nothing less than God's omnipotence is required to destroy it. I do nothing that is good if his omnipotence does not assist me. Satisfaction in one thing, vanity in another, justifications in another, esteem for myself, etc. In summary, in the end I find nothing but sins. Even in these gatherings of ours, I find a way to feed my pride by imagining that I am the reason for the good of all our wise sisters. (*Lett.* 60)[q]

And to her confessor, "My pride is very great, and so it makes me tremble to think that in the end it will yet remain victorious, and at every moment it seems to me that I am close to the precipice" (*Lett.* 65).[r]

To the same confessor, she revealed the anguish of her conflicting spiritual states of filial abandonment to God and the fear of deceiving herself:

> At times, there are inspirations so great that I, myself, recognize that I am very far from being able to fulfill them. On the contrary, it occurs to me quite often that I am deceived, that it is I who imagine these things in order to give greater reign to my pride; that I do no more than feign and put on an appearance, that the end of my work is not righteous, that in the end I will be among the damned, that I do no more than deceive myself and others, and similar things. Such thoughts cause me anxiety and fear, and so I do not know what to

---

[q] Capitanio to Cismondi, May 10, 1827, in *Scritti spirituali*, Letter 60.
[r] Capitanio to Bosio, July 12, 1827, in *Scritti spirituali*, Letter 65.

resolve. I would like to belong wholly to Jesus; I know that my pride stands in the way. All these thoughts make me believe that I am an object of revulsion to God so that I spend my days always between fear and hope, rejoicing a little and fearing a little, until the last day of my life comes, and they cannot take the thought from my mind that the day is close, and God knows what then will happen to me. (*Lett.* 73)[s]

To the Romelli sisters:

I beg you, dear sisters, recommend me to God. I do nothing other than work for the devil, and my works will serve only to greatly increase my hell, which I see always open for me under my feet. Believe me: if I do anything, I do it for no reason other than pride, and in my mind I esteem myself so greatly that I am persuaded even that my life will have to be written. For such pride and for countless, very tremendous sins, which I do not name in order not to scandalize you, I see my ruin close. (*Lett.* 78)[t]

In a very short note to her confessor, she chases herself into the most hidden corners:

Per your instruction, I confess that if you desire to humble me, what humbles me most is to point out to me some failure of pride noted above in the attached papers. And I tell you also that if you sometimes pointed out some particular failure in confession, such was the shame that I felt from it that I have never fallen again into the same fault. (*Lett.* 261)[u]

Perhaps this truly disconcerting dialectic regarding the most important and most difficult Christian virtue reached its summit in another letter, dated January 21, at 7 o'clock at night, but without indication of the year, which she sent to her confessor along with the papers of her examination of conscience:

To complete what is found in them, it is fitting to tell you something, which owing to my own pride, I have never been able to say out loud, and that is that I am proud because I wish to be so, because I love it, even though I ask the Lord often for holy humility; yet, I do not really

---

[s] Capitanio to Bosio, September 19, 1827, in *Scritti spirituali*, Letter 73.
[t] Capitanio to the Romellis, October 19, 1827, in *Scritti spirituali*, Letter 78.
[u] Capitanio to Bosio, n.d., in *Scritti spirituali*, Letter 261.

> desire it and I also frequently neglect the occasions for humiliation that present themselves to me. And do not think that I tell you these things with the end and feeling of humility; no, rather I tell them to you in pride, thinking that in this way I will have you regard me as humble. Yet, I recognize that this is a most necessary virtue, and so I am in continuous fear for my eternal salvation. (*Lett.* 273)[v]

This unspeakable suffering intensified and took the form of a melancholy, which is proper to the saints, and which has nothing in common with the pathology of a depressed conscience, the "spleen" of the poets, or that sinking into infinity to which great philosophers are prone, especially the metaphysicians. Hers is the affliction of moving away from that Good for whom she burns with love. Again, she writes to Cismondi:

> I confess to you that for two days I have suffered from a sadness so great that I could hardly control my tears. This was caused by my pride (I say it to you simply and as a sister) so that I greatly feared being abandoned by God, and it seemed to me that at any moment I would fall into grave sins that would have been a just chastisement for my pride. (*Lett.* 80)[w]

Nor was she spared that anxiety, that is, the radical melancholy, which seems to empty the spirit even of awareness of self. She described it in the admirable letter to her confessor, already cited:

> Last night, a certain affliction came into my heart that I have never experienced before. It started at the very moment when I made my confession, and so I was compelled to break into sighs, tears, and prayers. I felt an anxiety inside that troubled me greatly, but I did not know the reason for it. I slept only a little during the night and this, too, was bitter. As soon as I woke up, tears were in my eyes, sighs in my heart, as well as agitation; even while praying and during Holy Communion, involuntary tears continued to flow, without me knowing why, and so I asked the Lord several times: But, my God, what is happening? (*Lett.* 64)

However, as she added once she has regained her serenity, Our Lady came to her aid as if by an action arranged between heaven and earth, between the Virgin and her confessor:

---

[v] Capitanio to Bosio, January 21, in *Scritti spirituali*, Letter 273.
[w] Capitanio to Cismondi, November 2, 1827, in *Scritti spirituali*, Letter 80.

Several times, it occurred to me to seek recourse to Mary, but I was ashamed to do so because I had treated her very poorly. I almost did not dare to look at her . . .

But Mary does not pay attention to the faults of her daughters; she loves and supports them as a tender mother, even when they have been disloyal and unfaithful. This morning, as soon as I entered my room, I looked at her image, and it seemed to me that she looked kindly upon me, but still I continued in my abjection. When Your Reverence sent me the instruction to do something for Mary, only then was I truly consoled. It seemed as if Mary was saying to me, "I wish you to serve me." All my suffering disappeared immediately . . .

Now, I am joyful and happy. (*Lett.* 64)

Accordingly, the heroic sincerity, sweet spirit, and great intelligence of this privileged creature, which are the touching source of these letters, are so well reflected that we must regret that not a few of her letters seem to have been lost (e.g., the very long one written to her principal teacher, Mother Parpani, which she mentions in a letter to her confessor). During Capitanio's short life, her martyrdom seems to have been wholly spiritual; an exceptional soul, she found and carried out her struggle within the deep regions of the spirit. Her letters hardly mention, and barely even hint at, her external struggles or the opposition that her work generated. We find nothing about her temptations regarding fascination with temporal things (*fascinatio nugacitatis*) which have caused so much grief to so many souls, even the better ones. Rare are the hints about her physical suffering, about the continual fluctuations in her health that must have caused her bitter pain and unpleasant difficulties. The core of her struggle and of her holiness lies in the empyrean of her "subjectivity," in the sphere of that dominating "ego" that she had received from nature, which grace succeeded in transforming into a powerful instrument for good in order to bring to term the great enterprise to which God had destined her. Hers was a life without sudden dramas or great deeds. There is no claim that she performed any of those extraordinary actions that seem almost requisite in the life of founders. Even the miracles after her death have always been limited to the strictly necessary. But the miracle of her interior struggle will console with its light all who, like Capitanio, must wrestle "until dawn" with the invisible archangel of the I, where the only sign of victory is in finding oneself, like Jacob, limping and always more full of pain.

Vincenza Gerosa

THE LADY OF CHARITY

It was Gerosa herself who said of her angelic companion and co-foundress of the Sisters of Charity, whom we now call Sisters of the Holy Child Mary: "Capitanio is an eagle; I am an ox."[a] In her habitually tractable and pragmatic style, she unknowingly traces the program and secret of the mission of the Institute that God willed them to found. Perhaps never in the rich flowering of the Church's religious families did the fusion between the ardor of divine union and the outpouring of Christian charity have a character more frank or a fulfillment so integral. Were they to be encountered separately, these two souls would almost seem to be contraries. Capitanio has ready intuition, spiritual energy, and the sort of appeal that is present in youth; Gerosa has ponderous consideration, persistent diffidence toward herself and her work, and the profound fear of never fulfilling the divine request. The first is a volcano of initiatives and works that draws both the small and the great, worldly persons and priests, within its luminous orbit; born with a pen in her hand, with the most spontaneous rhythm, Capitanio writes sublime encouragements and pained supplications. The second seems to follow along her companion's path of light almost warily, immersing herself in self-forgetfulness through an unbounded dedication to the demands of charity, that which is most humble, most hidden, and apparently most insignificant. This, however, is a purely superficial impression and, in my opinion, betrays a very shallow evaluation of phenomena, which to our curious eyes have such sacred and mysterious value as does the spiritual structure of a religious family. Were one to say now that both the spirit and works of the Congregation of the Sisters of

---

[a] Cf. Gaetano Scandella, *Memorie intorno alla vita di Suor Vincenza Gerosa al secolo Caterina* (Brescia: Pio istituto dei figli di Maria, 1862), 118.

the Holy Child Mary take more after the good "Caterina"[b] Gerosa, his judgment would not be correct. The two saints devised the plan of the Institute together and it is not without reason that, having withdrawn to the Little Convent to begin their work, Capitanio loved to call Gerosa, "my good Superior!"

In the first place, they were united in meeting the Institute's initial and immediate need for material and legal stability. Each disposed of all her possessions by donating them to the new Congregation. Gerosa's sizeable wealth formed the principal part of the Congregation's patrimony. She had to struggle and wait for many years to overcome the obstinate incomprehension of a difficult aunt in order to make her generous bequest. Capitanio's own collection of letters tells us about the sufferings, as well as the tenacious perseverance of her companion, who won out in the end. They were united in their program of charity: the Christian education of young girls and aid to the sick. The absolute dedication to these two aims had its birth precisely in the Little Convent, and it is according to the same foundational spirit that even today the Congregation, whose generous embrace has extended to the whole world, continues to achieve these two ends to the benefit of innumerable souls. They were united in suffering the initial oppositions and difficulties of every kind that were meant to stop them. They were also united by the understandable anguish of being separated just at the most critical time because of the sudden, premature death of the bold young woman to whom the original idea of the work was due. When Capitanio, barely twenty-six, left this earth on April 26, 1833, everyone expected the dissolution of their difficult enterprise, but docile to the subtle prompting of her superiors, Gerosa put herself to work. Straightaway, she strove successfully to conclude the process of obtaining legal recognition from the government, which she received along with fundamental assurances. To the merit of the same Gerosa, she called Maria Gallini to her aid, first as a substitute for Capitanio in the school, during the final assault of the illness that put an end to Capitanio's precious life, and later as faithful secretary and interpreter.

Some other souls formed at Capitanio's school, whom Gerosa first welcomed, were Chiara Colombo, Margherita Rivellini, and Francesca Rosa. If others in that first nucleus formed by the young foundress did not feel the strength to continue with Gerosa, nevertheless, spiritual

---

[b] "Catterina" in *Profili di Santi*.

continuity was assured thanks to the largeness of spirit and the immensity of this good peasant woman's trust in God. Though lacking letters and studies, she was entirely filled with good sense and expert in the practice of boundless dedication to the cause of God. Where the divine will was concerned, she did not back down in the face of difficulties that would have caused even the most resolute wills to totter. With trembling in her heart and tears in her eyes, she agreed to give her daughters for the most delicate and difficult apostolates, entrusting everything to the God who had called them to bring the light of faith in the Institute for admonition and correction of Venice. Despite certain appearances to the contrary, the depth of her insight was obvious; as when because of the political situation, she granted the community of the Ospedale Maggiore [Great Hospital] of Milan, as well as the new foundations within the diocese of Milan and throughout Lombardy, the semi-autonomous governance on which they would rely to ensure the normal functioning of their work. It is thanks to Gerosa's great tact that, when the conditions of the times had changed, the Institute was able to reunite as one family without conflicts or lasting consequences, and with that same spirit and program that we can still admire even now in the grandeur of the shared glory of its two founding saints.

Then again, the interior spirit and path to holiness of Capitanio and Gerosa was the same as well: the complete annihilation of self through a boundless dedication to the assistance of neighbor. Perhaps the only difference is that, while we know from her collection of letters the bitter struggle that Capitanio had to wage in order to gain victory over her ego, for Gerosa the practice of humility flowed according to a natural rhythm, as if from a pure spring. Gerosa's humility had unusual traits and a disconcerting radicality not often found even in the lives of very well-known saints. Her humility was total and without reservation, regarding herself and everything surrounding her, regarding her person and the very notion of her work. Foreign to her were the distinctions that we religious make, namely that of finding a certain exaltation of our Congregations consistent and correct, while believing that we leave intact the practice of personal humility. Such pitiful cavils, which often unmask a more powerful pride, were the polar opposite of the evangelical sentiment *sine glossa* of this great soul. Her whole life is evidence of this humility. She loved the humblest tasks. Toward her daughters, she practiced such boundless dedication that, in certain circumstances, not even a mother could ever have conceived or have been able to imagine it. She held herself in contempt naturally and adopted the most unassuming demeanor.

Like St. Philip, she carried out gestures of holy folly in order to become contemptible to all, especially when she saw that she was held in high regard or when she was visited by important people. In July 1842, when the Archduke of Austria came to visit her in Lovere, he found her in the kitchen with a rag as her apron; it was in that attire that she wished to present herself to him.

The "little flowers of St. Gerosa" would constitute a document of high spiritual value as well as a jewel of hagiographical literature. It would be necessary to gather and catalogue her sayings, her answers, her quick and sure decisions. In her natural and kindly expression shines a heavenly light together with the awareness of a self-annihilation so joyful and pure that it brings to mind the ascetical classics of the golden age of Christian monasticism. Her words and decisions were "always blunders"; when the work succeeded, she was "good for nothing" and someone else was responsible. In her whole life, she had done "no good at all," and should God grant her "a little corner in Paradise, by his pure mercy," or should he place her "behind the door," it would be too much for her.[c] She confessed that "I have more fear of praise than the devil because the devil can be chased away with the sign of the cross, while praise lingers to harm the soul!" With feelings of great simplicity and compunction, she went so far as to ask a sister to "Do me an act of charity and quiz me about the principal mysteries of the holy faith, the Persons of the Most Holy Trinity and other things, because I fear that I have forgotten them."[d] What is more, when someone thanked her for her prayers, attributing to them favors obtained from heaven, she interrupted and said, "But I have had no part in it, because I have even forgotten to pray!" She regarded herself as unworthy of any regard. Even in her last illness, she never became accustomed to better treatment, complaining as though she were excessively delicate for finding herself in bed and surrounded with necessary assistance. She met her death serenely as one seized by a holy haste and impatience to be joined with the Highest Good.

She did not want her Congregation to be praised because she feared that it would assume an air of exterior prestige and accomplishment; therefore, she evinced great reluctance in accepting members with diplomas and those who came from distinguished families. She would defend herself saying, "We are poor, little women; you are not suited to us. Our

---

[c] Cf. Giovanni Colombo, "Pensieri sui Vangeli di Luglio," *La Rivista del Clero Italiano* 18, no. 7 (July 1937): 397.

[d] Cf. Colombo, "Pensieri": 397.

Institute is too lowly for you." She would repeat often: "Our Institute is nothing; it is the least of all."[e] To requests for new foundations, she responded that her sisters were good for nothing. When the Archbishop of Milan praised them, as if offended, she said, "Chastise them! Chastise them!"[f] When the Bishop of Trent, the Venerable Msgr. Johann Tschiderer,[g] asked for sisters for the hospital, alluding to the small number of sisters who had made profession that year, she responded, "This year's brood has been bad!"

Thus, her soul was a living mirror of that sort of genuine Christian wisdom, which is the principal characteristic of strong souls. She was never willing to believe that any external status could excuse one from seeking the deepest abnegation and complete annihilation of self. However, this was not pusillanimity nor pettiness. She knew how to be magnanimous when it was necessary and showed that if one wishes to do everything for God and for souls, he should not exempt himself from principles binding on all. Once, when one of her employees had disobeyed her, she asked emphatically, "Is this the love you have for your mistress?" Coming from her lips, such an uncharacteristic way of speaking was striking; it betrayed a personality that was rooted in her family's affluence. The total sacrifice that she made to God of that innate lack of pretention made this small betrayal all the more precious and moving.

This profound humility was watered at the deepest springs of the supernatural life and of her union with God. Her fervor, which was suffused with a Franciscan simplicity that had become connatural with her spirit, radiated from her with the magisterial authority of invincible attractiveness. The sister who cared for her in her last illness attested that she always made two meditations during the night and more throughout the day. The ones at night lasted an hour. When her illness caused her greater suffering, she would have someone read some point or other from the Lord's Passion and as she listened to the recounting, she would lament with affection: "Jesus is on the Cross, and yet here am I comfortable in a good bed. Lord, forgive my excessive delicacy and let me suffer, for I am a sinner!"[h]

---

[e] Cf. Scandella, *Memorie*, 73 f.
[f] Cf. Scandella, *Memorie*, 102.
[g] "Tschiederer" in *Profili di Santi*.
[h] Cf. Scandella, *Memorie*, 131.

Selfsame was the exceptional spiritual energy of the two holy foundresses, selfsame their yearning to be immolated for the Divine Spouse and for the relief of those who suffer, and selfsame the intent to plunge into the abyss of their own nothingness.

Maria Goretti

CONSCIOUS OF INNOCENCE

A martyr is one who gives the "testimony of blood." Martyrdom gains the most intimate conformity with Christ through the shedding of the blood with which the tyrant clothes the victim, who is presented to God for the highest glorification. Consequently, when freedom is understood as being completely apparent and conscious, martyrdom becomes, by a strange paradox, more immense and more intimate than freedom itself. It seems as if Providence, in its mysterious counsels, does not always wait for a flower to reach the glory of full bloom; but rather, at times, decides to steal it away from the light untouched, picking it as a tightly furled bud still jealously guarding its splendor. The Holy Innocents were such unknowing martyrs, destroyed by a tyrant like roses yet to bloom, having only just opened their tender petals to the light of the world that here below they were unable either to choose or to know. Almost at the extreme opposite stand those martyrs who in this life were sinners and who, by an unfathomable decree of grace, washed away the failures of their fragile nature with their own blood. Yet, if we may say so, truly first class martyrdom lies in an ineffable synthesis of the two, which is the martyrdom of conscious innocence. In it, the brightness of the lily is not simply an accident of unwitting nature, but the anxious conquest of each day. The context of the call to immolation is not, then, a reparation for past weaknesses, but rather the brightness of a conquest of perfect purity in fidelity to God. It is also for this reason that the Church, filled with wonder by such a prodigy, reserves to the holy virgins and martyrs in the heavenly Jerusalem such an imcomparable glory as surpasses every ideal exaltation of woman, whether it be in the classical world or in romantic idealism.

In the case of Maria Goretti, the striking traits of this consciousness of martyrdom are verified by testimonies so rich and consistent that they reveal, in turn, the Divine Spirit's mysterious plan of predilection regarding this innocent and blessed girl. The unspeakable sufferings of poverty—the wretched torments of which reached their worst with the death of the head of the family—showed her early on that essential aspect of sacrifice which life must have for every Christian conscience. Even so, there is still more to Goretti. In the *Summary* of the Apostolic Processes, the witnesses agree regarding the precocious and harmonious nature of her physical development. What they found immediately striking was the light of grace, of serenity, and of maturity conferred on her small frame by the fulfillment of hard daily labor in an environment that ought to have done away with every higher aspiration. Furthermore, these witnesses, beginning with her mother, draw attention to the exceptional strength of soul that, in the moments of greatest distress, had the capacity to console even her mother. The latter also says that Maria seemed to have dominion over nature itself because, when she went to work in the fields, the snakes, lizards, and vipers never troubled her, but instead disappeared immediately, as if dazed and defeated by her gentle emergence. The early development of nature and grace was what prepared her for the ultimate sacrifice. Undoubtedly, she had a clear perception of sin, as well as a holy horror of saddening that Spirit who transforms the bodies of the souls that welcome him into living temples of his mysterious, loving presence. To those who, after her cruel death, claimed that it was not possible for a girl of twelve to be aware of that sin, her mother Assunta has always replied, almost disdainfully, "But these people never knew Maria. They don't know what happened and they have little or no religion."

No one was able to attest to the reality of the facts better than Alessandro Serenelli. Struck by grace, Alessandro himself has given the most detailed and most definitive witness of Maria's innocence and fortitude by testifying to the girl's tenacious resistance to his earlier attempts. Furthermore, we learn from him that while he, enraged as he was by her last refusal, struck the fatal blows on that innocent body, she ("the pitiful, the unfortunate girl," as the royal procurator says in his report) did not even try to ward off the blows that pierced her, but was concerned only with covering herself. Consequently, the surgeon who carried out the autopsy reassured her fearful mother, "Have no doubt; she is as she was born!" The consciousness of innocence that had become the atmosphere of her soul was so perfect that, even in the delirium of imminent death, it compelled her to a painful but triumphant repetition of the terrible exchange during the struggle that cast her down in her own blood. "Alessandro, what are you doing?—No, no! God does not will it. . . . If you do this, you will go to hell!" Already gripped by a cruel death, the innocent soul opened up in its "inner form," and poured out a charity of commiseration. She, the small pierced victim, "trampled down like corn," as Serenelli would say, was the one who dispenses the graces for which she generously prayed. After overcoming the initial torment and the natural fear that produced the horrified cry, "Mother, I am dying!" her pure countenance was composed and her few remaining words were words of consolation for her desolate mother: "Mother, do not cry. I am well!" Then from her lips blossomed forgiveness, "I forgive him, and I hope that God will forgive him also."

Without a doubt, the most energetic assertion of the martyrdom of Maria Goretti came from Alessandro Serenelli. At first, at the instigation of bigoted lawyers, he lied, yet he did not escape the maximum penalty to which a minor could be sentenced (he spent twenty-seven years in prison). It was in this place of expiation, isolated from the fellowship of other men, that he found the path to salvation in a return to God. It was Maria, his poor victim, who pointed the path out to him. "I dreamed of Maria, all dressed in white, gathering the whitest of lilies in a garden and handing them to me one by one and saying: 'Take them!' As she gave them to me, they all became bright lights and then she disappeared." After returning to his senses and the practice of religion, Serenelli never ceased to proclaim the unclouded virtue of his victim. After he was released, he was not satisfied until he had detailed the absolute innocence of the girl in the most minute and most horrific terms. He told the ecclesiastical authorities who sought his testimony, "It is my duty. I must make reparation and do all in my power for her glorification. The wrong was entirely mine because I let myself be blinded by a brutal passion. She was right to to preserve her innocence by resisting. She was truly an innocent girl. In those days," he added thoughtfully in a tone of deep sadness at the memory of a youth so tragically wasted in the squalor of prison, "children were not as they are now. Back then, they were simple and good, especially in the countryside. Maria was truly good and in order to preserve her purity, she preferred to fall under the hand of a murderer (!). Therefore, the fault was entirely mine." He concluded: "If there are martyrs in Paradise, she is the first among them! . . . With all I did to her!" At the time that she was martyred, the innocent victim had been mending one of Serenelli's shirts; when she reached Heaven, she wished to mend his soul, and sought for him the mercy of Christian repentance. His conversion was the fruit of her intercession and of a heavenly presence that became, little by little, ever more intense and luminous in his heart—the same heart that had remained deaf to even the most imploring pleas of his wounded victim and even to the protest of the very blood that sought his pity.

This martyrdom of conscious innocence is the prodigy of the heroism of the simple; once more, "has not God made foolish the wisdom of the world?" (1 Cor 1:20). Maria Goretti was a poor, illiterate country girl, forced to the harsh labors of her household. The fundamental truths of faith illuminated the clear heaven of her soul, without distractions, not even the simplest reference to a child's primer or a book of fables, without experiencing the enchantment of the mystery of being or of the adventure of the world to which, in either small or great measure, each of us yielded at the school desks of childhood. Docile to her inner voice, the girl did not need an abstract and secondhand "conception of the world." Since her mother had to take care of the work in the fields, she lived her days under the urgency of the sacrifice of an eldest daughter upon whom weighed the care of the household and assistance to her younger siblings. "All lay on Maria's shoulders," her mother would say. Yet Maria was ever ready and quick, as though she did not feel her tiredness. All affirm that she was of few words, but she was always well mannered and helpful toward all, even to Serenelli after his first advances. When she did her meager shopping, she was quite capable of taking careful accounts at the store; she caused wonder with her easy and self-assured bearing which was so unusual for one of her condition. And as she walked away, the eyes of the simple people of the countryside, who know how to discern and savor virtue and grace, followed her with deep satisfaction, as though she were a present glorification of their humble condition. Maria, being entirely recollected, always returned home with a hurried step without ever stopping with anyone.

Never did this holy martyr have even the slightest leisure to indulge her spiritual life. It is well known that she thirsted for religious instruction, which she retained very well in her mind, and that she diligently attended catechism classes at the cost of great sacrifice. It was more difficult for her to approach Holy Communion, which she received for the first time only a month before her martyrdom. Throughout that month, she was only able to approach the Sacrament of Love perhaps three times. Just as in the first centuries of the Church, when the Christian, by means of baptism and with the first approach to the mystery of the Body and

Blood of Christ, was as if consecrated for the martyrdom that almost always awaited. In like manner, having been educated exclusively at the wisdom of the cross, the young Maria Goretti left all of us behind, presumptuous as we are, living in a culture and civilization that renders us each day ever more deaf to God's call.

The Little Flowers of Sister Bertilla

It seemed that this most humble daughter of the people lacked any natural talent. At first glance, almost no one had any trust in her. The chaplain in her native town of Brendola did not believe her capable of holding any office in the community. The perplexed Mistress of Novices did not believe her fit for anything other than physical labor in the kitchen, laundry, or scullery. And such was the impression of insignificance conveyed by her weak body and unassuming demeanor, that her first frustrated superior at the hospital in Treviso did not know what task to entrust her. However, then God allowed the obstacles to fall away. During Holy Mass, the chaplain received an inspiration and notified the young Anna, barely an adolescent, of his consent to her entrance into religious life. Little by little—unconsciously—the superiors and the sisters began, mostly because of the fascination they experienced in face of that most heroic sacrifice, to feel the presence of an ineffable grace in the humble religious, like that of a heavenly gift.

Yet Sr. Bertilla herself seemed to almost have been in collusion with this plot to make her struggle in darkness, forgetfulness, and contempt because she accepted all manner of unpleasant reproofs, complaints, and judgments from everyone, including superiors, sisters, and quarrelsome patients. When she was insulted by being reckoned a "goose," a "poor blockhead," a "dimwit," a "good for nothing," or even more disparaging names, she would agree. "Yes, indeed, I am a blockhead! . . . You are right. Forgive me, Mother Superior. I will try to make you happy." Moreover, she made this confession while kneeling humbly before those who humiliated her. Guided only by the Divine Spirit, this very simple soul became so hidden that she revealed herself only to those who recognized the motions of her purest love for God and for her suffering neighbor. In this way, by providential circumstance, she was appointed to offices that required great care and responsibility: to assist in the hospital of Treviso in the department for children with infectious diseases, in the department for those with tuberculosis, and finally in operating room number 24. In this setting, not only did she perform her duties so as to give complete satisfaction, but revealed an intuition, tact, readiness that astonished even the physicians who could no longer do without her. This victory might have secured her some respectable position. Instead, the humble sister used it as a new occasion to offer herself as a substitute to relieve the other sisters, even though she was the most tired, having already been afflicted for more than ten years by the illness that would lead to her early death.

Yet the complete purification of this privileged soul occurred at the military sanatorium of Viggiù at the beginning of the First World War. An impressive number of reports in the *Summarium* recount the humanly incomprehensible nature of the incident with a troubling realism that moves us to shuddering indignation. The superior, who was surly, suspicious, and impossible to satisfy, chose Sr. Bertilla as the object of her ceaseless and shameless outbursts of irrational temper. Even in the obvious face of the terrible pain and physical ruin consuming the poor victim, she was mercilessly subjected to the pitiless tactics of systematic persecution and to storms of insults and humiliations. One need only recall the repugnant scene unleashed by the episode of the diapers fallen in the courtyard. As if this were not enough, even after her death the aforementioned superior continued her persecution in the hypocrisy of her first canonical deposition. It incited the just wrath of the inquiring prelate. Her duplicity and wrath were recorded later in a supplementary report, the existence of which is a testimony to the maternal solicitude displayed by the Church in defense of the unstained flowers of Her Mystical Body. In any case, Sr. Bertilla extracted her retribution, a saintly vengeance. When that same wretched superior, who had fallen ill, invoked her intercession, she was healed immediately and her hard heart was softened. This led to an act of retraction that while tardy was an acknowledgment of the debt due the saint. Yet, it is clear that Sr. Bertilla never protested nor did she judge the deeds of her superiors, whom she respected without distinction. The kind words she received from her Mother General filled her with unspeakable joy—a joy expressed even on her deathbed when she saw beside her the one who, for her faith, was God himself.

The secret of such a radiant devotion to God remained hidden from impious eyes. For the most part—as in the case of St. Thérèse of the Child Jesus, to whom Bertilla was very devoted—her sisters seemed unaware of the very great gift given to them by God. They had called her "a poor wretch," and she echoed it with delight, taking for herself only that food, clothing, and daily work that no one else was willing to bear or to wear. Yet something still filtered through of the holy fire that consumed her soul, and which through intense contact, drew even her body toward its end. Hers was the seraphic fervor of unconditional dedication to a life of authentic martyrdom. At the same time, Sr. Bertilla's piety is of the most transparent and heroic kind: she breathed the air of supernatural life like normal air and for this reason her life brooked no delays, no contrasts. The presence of God and devotion to the Passion and to the Eucharist drew from her sighs and cries of holy compassion and guileless joy in the mysteries of faith. After Holy Communion, her face became transfigured with a beauty that edified those present, yet some of the sisters smiled at this, convinced that it confirmed that Sr. Bertilla's intelligence and her ability were below average. However, the marvel of her mission became evident, on both the physical and moral planes, through her dedication to duties in departments where death and suffering rend bodies with fearsome violence. Her presence alone generated trust and both patients and physicians strenuously sought her assistance. It was in moments when all seemed lost that this substandard sister, who seemed destined to be forgotten and despised, would step forward with a good idea as to the best remedy, which was infused in her by the vigor of charity. This lent to her the charm of a will that seemed destined to emerge victorious in such moments of extreme pleas. Anyone who wishes to study the deep theological roots of Sr. Bertilla's sanctity must consider this miracle, one that no psychology will ever be able to explain.

Therefore, it is not surprising that it was the physicians and patients whom she assisted, before her own sisters, who first began the glorification of Sr. Bertilla. They are the ones who mourned and cried for her when she died. They are the ones who praised her in public and in private, who gave the first votive offerings, and they who wished her life to be written. God reserved for these worldly people, some of whom did not even practice religion, the fragrance of this purest of flowers. Their simple depositions contain the fierceness and joy that go with the privilege of making such an incomparable discovery. Let the testimony of Count Ferruccio Zuccardi, the medical director of the hospital of Treviso, under whom she served as head nurse of the surgical department and by whom, in a desperate attempt to save her life, she was persuaded to undergo her last operation, stand for all. He testified:

> She has always given me the impression that there was something outside of her, a being that prompted and guided her, because she was a person who, in her mission of piety and charity, always rose above those who lived under the same laws and acted under the same tension, toward the same end of religious life. Considered materially, she had no qualities of intelligence or culture that made her superior to the others, yet she truly gave the impression of being moved, almost automatically, according to the action of a higher being, of an angel who might be leading her. It is impossible for a physician to think of a person who, like Sr. Bertilla, spends one, two, fifteen sleepless nights, and yet always appears the same, unconcerned for herself, without ever giving a hint of her exhaustion or of the illness that consumed her and not admit that there was, I repeat, something that, as it were, elevated her either from the inside or from the outside.

Notice how effective is the peace and consolation, which results from this spiritual appeal:

> Imagine, for example, the case of a little girl who, after overcoming her illness, was discharged from the hospital. . . . Her parents, well, her mother waits at the door for the healed little one; and at that moment, a sudden attack of acute myocarditis kills the child almost instantaneously. It is impossible to imagine the despair into which the spirits of those poor parents, of that poor mother, fall. Yet, the Servant of God possessed such virtue, such efficacy, that she was able to convince those parents to accept the event with resignation. For me, all this constitutes the externalization of a plexus of virtues such as is difficult to imagine.

Picture the mother of the little children who suffer:

> Some children with diphtheria were brought to the department. They were torn away from their families and thus they were in a state of such agitation and despair that they could not be easily calmed. For two or three days, they behaved like little animals: hitting,

striking, hiding under the bed, refusing to eat, etc. Yet, the Servant of God was rapidly able to become like a mother to all of them. After two or three hours, a formerly desolate child was calmed and clung to her as though to its mother's skirt, and accompanied her as she went about her tasks. Under the influence of the Servant of God, the department presented the moving sight of a clump of children attached to her: a truly exemplary department!

All it took to induce the children to immediately stop their crying and to become docile and calm was to tell them that Sr. Bertilla would go away if they were not good and obedient. She exercised the spiritual attraction that she possessed in an even more profound manner on those patients who were the most ill and those who were the most removed from God. She was the only one whom they were unable to resist.

The many tears that Sr. Bertilla shed in the course of her short life were seen as both faults and flaws. Her soul's sweetness provided no defensive barriers against the harshness of life and the human egotism that was unleashed upon her. She cried inconsolably at the death of her mother and brother; she cried over the sins of the world and the offenses made to God, and also over the sudden troubles that continued to descend upon her, because she truly feared being the cause of disdain for others. She prepared for her own death, of which she had a presentiment, with serenity and joy as though for her own wedding banquet, often repeating the maxim of high mystical wisdom, which was her favorite: "Everything is nothing . . . To see the Lord, it is necessary to die."

"Poor Gemma"

ON THE FIFTIETH ANNIVERSARY OF HER DEATH (1953)

The saints are given to us in order to console and incite us. Though, for a while, they appear to walk in stride with us, at a certain point, the impetus of divine attraction seems to set them at such a distance that it is impossible to see them as still being within the same sphere as our own temporal existence. Henceforth, we are left without any gauge by which to judge a life whose principle of movement is drawn from somewhere else, from the very depths of Providence. Moreover, if each saint fulfills a particular function in building up of the Mystical Body of the Church, often, he does so in the manner of one who walks in darkness. God wills that nature be broken in the life of reason, which is the core of autonomy, and the saints often walk in the darkness of the purifying tension of faith, making a total sacrifice of the ego and of all those offshoots which modern culture has conceived of under the sumptuous term of personality. Feeling new and ineffable impressions, it would seem to the soul that the entire array of virtues found in the *Nicomachean Ethics* had been placed under ban; it is beset by such awful doubts regarding its path and regarding the very truths of faith that it asks itself how this can be reconciled with the presence of grace. To suffer simultaneously both the greatest attraction toward and the strongest revulsion for the Infinite Good, and to be pulled by parallel but opposing motivations is surely the most disconcerting experience that a creature can have of the divine. In the case of those saints who have left us direct testimony of this struggle with the invisible, the essential reference points of which are in the Agony in the Garden of Gethsemane and the abandonment of Christ on the Cross, these contradictions assume features that shake and trouble us.

In Gemma Galgani's case, these disconcerting aspects of a shattered personality have reached a level of exasperation, as it were, which has few equals in Catholic spirituality. Everything is turned upside down and goes awry in her life, something that she herself reveals to us in an artless and continuous dialogue. Yet, what is most striking is that the contradictions, the setbacks, and the darkness did not come from without, nor were they simply worldly struggles or resistance in her nature. They came from God himself. Throughout her life, he seemed to suspend her soul from a thread of ambiguity that appears to prevent any resolution of what had yet been her obvious intention to give herself to God.

It could be said that this test of the annihilation of the ego in Gemma's life took place in two failing directions: on one side were the supernatural events by which she was always surrounded, and on the other, the drama of her religious vocation. The profusion of the supernatural in her life, which bordered on the incredible, sharpens for us the problem inherent in the possibility of human experiences of divine things. Her guardian angel, the Savior, St. Gabriel of Our Lady of Sorrows, and the Blessed Virgin Mary were all habitual confidants and counselors for Gemma. She was able to speak with them, to receive their guidance and the marks of their affection, on a supernatural level that seemed to her to be part of ordinary life. Throughout almost all of her life, which consisted entirely in pleading for and in accepting suffering for the salvation of sinners, are threaded such rare mystical phenomena as discernment of spirits and a direct physical participation in the sufferings of Christ's Passion. Meanwhile, in contrast, she suffered terrifying physical and moral demonic vexations that bordered on torment. Even now, when we read of these things, whenever the secret world of the spirit is torn open and that obscure mystery of the evil which has bound human existence from its origin, is exposed, it causes us to shudder in horror. Caught up as she was in such great things, Gemma did not presume to rely on nor to trust in herself, but instead recounted everything to her spiritual director with guileless candor.

Standing against this frank openness of her simple and translucent soul was the authority of her confessor, the very pious Msgr. Volpi, who seems never to have accepted the supernatural character of these manifestations in his humble penitent. However, Gemma continued to confess these manifestations, which she attributed only to her own "head." Her only fear was to deceive and to be deceived: "Monsignor, help me not to deceive myself. I do not wish for these visions; I would only like that

Jesus forgive me those things, as you know" (*Lett.* 34).ª "As for all these things, I regard them as you wish me to do. I have written to you first of all in order to obey Jesus, and then, when you know everything, I feel lighter" (*Lett.* 54).ᵇ Also, "Forgive me and do not yell at me; I do not believe in them, because I know that my imagination is capable of anything" (*Lett.* 64).ᶜ Her confessor's policy of doubt, certainly inspired by solid theological prudence, was an invaluable guardian for Gemma's humility, and for that reason a decisive factor in her sanctity. Had it been any other soul, it might have unleashed one of those storms that raze the spiritual edifice to the ground.

Equally or perhaps even more fierce was the drama of her vocation. Willingly would Gemma have renounced everything, including her visions and ecstasies, if it had been granted to her to retire to "be a slave," and a "servant of all," among the Passionist Sisters. If there is one mandate in her visions that was explicit, continuous, and peremptory, it was that Gemma would be, that she had to become, a Passionist religious. Indeed, during a vision in December 1899, St. Gabriel of Our Lady of Sorrows categorically reassured her: "You shall be a Passionist; these are God's words and they shall not fail" (*Lett.* 19 to Msgr. Volpi). As a daughter of the Passion, she was certainly the object of a most singular predilection, but not in the way that she desired and glimpsed in her visions. During the last months of her life, exhausted by illness, even her mental faculties wavered as she watched every hope of the convent fade away. This bewilderment, almost dejection, speaks to the immensity of the spiritual pains that purified this most sensitive and delicate creature. In terms of robust theology, this was the supreme test of total renunciation for which Gemma had prepared herself: "But is this peace in my heart? Is this tranquility in my soul?—No, I do not want the assurance; I wish to live in your holy fear" (*Estasi* 125).ᵈ Even so, the deep suffering still seeped out: "Come, come; then I will worry about the rest . . . Were I but a little certain of being in your grace, O Lord!" (*Estasi* 136).ᵉ In addition, barely

---

ª Gemma Galgani to Giovanni Volpi, June 1900. Cf. *Lettere di S. Gemma Galgani* (Rome: Postulazione dei PP. Passionisti, 1941).

ᵇ Galgani to Volpi, March 1901.

ᶜ Galgani to Volpi, March 1902.

ᵈ Ecstasy, August 18, 1902. Cf. *Estasi, diario, autobiografia, scritti vari di S. Gemma Galgani* (Rome: Postulazione dei PP. Passionisti, 1943).

ᵉ Ecstasy, November 18, 1902.

a year before her death, she exclaims: "I am ashamed, O Jesus; I know that I am not on the right path. I must seek the way of the cross" (*Estasi* 86).[f]

The mission of Fr. Germanus of St. Stanislaus, the humble religious with a robust intellect (he was a good philosopher and a brilliant archeologist), who did so much for "poor Gemma" both during her life and after her death, should be understood in the context of this exceptional vocation to suffering. The letters that the girl from Lucca wrote to him constitute a document that is unique in Christian spirituality. Gemma's soul is a translucent crystal amid the fluctuations of her sufferings and joys. To her "*babbo*,"[g] she confided everything in a fresh manner of her angelic language, so different from that of St. Catherine of Siena. Never does Gemma use the peremptory "I want" (*voglio*), that commanding attitude of victorious archangel, proper to the great Dominican. Rather, there was humble waiting for further sufferings, sighs of Paradise, shivers of sorrow for the sins of the world, and especially a constant insecurity that made her desire the nearness of her "*buon babbo*" [good father], her God-given guide. These outbursts were innumerable: "I am always restless, always in search of a good that might calm me, that might console me, that might give me a little rest" (*Lett.* 92).[h] "Of course, He has always hidden from me the place where I should be" (*Lett.* 99).[i] In her thirst for humiliation, she went as far as siding with the critics of her extraordinary phenomena. She writes to Fr. Germanus: "Yes, indeed, (that religious person) knows me, but you do not and are mistaken. My things do not come from God, but everything comes from the devil. Pray to Jesus. Light, light, my father. It is all false devotion, as I see only too well; it is all hypocrisy" (*Lett.* 105).[j]

The spirituality of Gemma lies in this tender, trusting fortitude that fills her letters to her distant spiritual director. It is impossible to read them and not to be aware of the present reality of a new mercy, which God granted to man through the holiness of this virgin from Lucca. However, her piety was of the same cast and substance as the "Catherinian" one: "Sometimes, I think and say: 'But have you forgotten everything else, my God? Do you have nothing else to do than to behold

---

[f] Ecstasy, April 11, 1902.
[g] An affectionate term for father.
[h] Galgani to Fr. Germanus, December 7, 1901.
[i] Galgani to Germanus, January 28, 1902.
[j] Galgani to Germanus, March 8, 1902.

me?' And immediately a light forms in my mind: that Jesus, in the immutable light of his divine vision, does not grow by beholding only one person, me alone, nor does he diminish by looking at many creatures" (*Lett.* 111).[k]

For the incredulous Msgr. Volpi, the saint reserved the most disconcerting manifestation of her earthly mission and the prophecy of her glorification. This time, it concerned a "sensible" rather than an imaginary vision, according to the Thomistic terminology. It was March 1901, two years before her death, and the saint was speaking with the Child Jesus, whom she held on her lap: "O Jesus, now you will surely grant me the grace that I desire. Tomorrow, you will show Monsignor the truth." Jesus's extremely audacious answer was: "My daughter, as for the truth, the one who was supposed to know it (that is, Fr. Germanus) knows it; as for Monsignor, it is not yet time for him to know it, but the time will come when he will know it. Assure him that it is I, Jesus, who speak to you, and that in a few years, by my work, you will be a saint, will do miracles, and will be raised to the honors of the altar" (*Lett.* 55 to Msgr. Volpi). There is enough here to turn our whole school theology upside down. . . .

Gemma's future mission in the life of the Church still lies hidden in these letters, as well as in the sorrows and joys that they reveal. At first glance, the spiritual life is presented as a harsh landscape full of rocks and impassable summits that are fearsome. However, this inexorable purification accomplished by God in innocent souls, to which we cannot be indifferent, serves to shed some light on the horror of sin and of the unappealing things of life. The spirituality issuing from these lines, so seemingy simple, so ringing with divine joys and pains, told as they are with childlike tenderness, has an essence that is metaphysical in the absolute sense. The only way of salvation is that of the cross; expiation for sinners must be offered by the innocent. It is difficult for us, stuffed as we are with cultural and technological knowledge, to understand this language, which is the message of Good Friday. We debate well about theology and even mysticism, and we can classify methods and schools of spirituality according to pertinent and refined distinctions and observations. Half a century ago, a true daughter of the people preferred instead to follow the way of the cross with such ardent love, in order to savor in the ineffable fragrance of the Blood of Christ, the sole certainty in which to live and hope.

---

[k] Galgani to Germanus, June 22, 1902.

The Humility and Greatness of Pope Sarto

After St. Pius V, four centuries passed during which the supreme glory open to a creature no longer came to rest on a Pope. In Pius X, the glory returned not only to continue the tradition of the Office and of the See which draws its very name and its exceptional mission from holiness, but also in order to carry out the recovery of "human equality." The Pope, who guides the Church in the way of truth with supreme Magisterium and, with an infallible judgment, holds up her best children as examples, remains a fragile creature, subject to the burden of daily misery and to the arduous play of earthly contingencies. Perhaps in no other human office do individual characteristics emerge to impose themselves with more evident significance as in the case of one who rises to this throne, which is the first in greatness, but which also imposes a measure of the superhuman on the creature who holds it. This is why no dynasty has ever offered such variety and multiplicity in the realization of the same ideal as has the Roman Pontificate. With the freedom of the children of God, in the fulfillment of his mission, the Pope leaves behind a unique imprint of himself that remains in the Church, and often even in the world, marking the passage of events that keep man in suspense. Before the world, the Church, and even himself, the man who comes to that pinnacle must look in the mirror without subterfuges, conscious that he expresses the highest essence of the life of the spirit. How much more admirable is it then, if amid so many hardships and difficulties, a Pope's life is purified by a simple spirit of supreme self-immolation, so that he is able to give, in himself, a living example of that same virtue regarding which he must judge others.

The call for the elevation of Pius X to sainthood first arose from the voice of the people. It is a joyous testimony to the unity of the Mystical Body. It is like a renewal of the presence of the humble and simple in the declaration of glory. This is because Pius X had made for himself an almost seamless tunic out of Christian humility and simplicity, which he alone knew how to wear with ease; and this garment grew with him as he grew in greatness. At each step of his ascent, this garment, far from becoming dimmed or forgotten, became more resplendent and gave a new and more frank witness of itself. Beyond simply remembering past sufferings, beyond being aware of having been born poor, of having had a troubled childhood, and of having completed his studies only with the aid of others, in this testimony of "being" poor he rediscovered a sort of spiritual "presence" within all the new dignities for which God destined him. By simple recognition of the evidence, the fact of the high intellect which put him always first among his peers, his sure judgment of men and events, his very ability to govern, and even the distinction of his exceptionally gifted nature, ought to have exempted him from what is now called an "inferiority complex." So it was for many historical figures—even for those in the Church—whose humble beginnings formed the backdrop, or even the "negative circumstances," against which the greatness achieved is highlighted by contrast and with even greater emphasis. Pius X was the son of a tax collector, the second of numerous siblings. His humble origins and the anxiety caused by want of even the basic necessities of life was transformed into his very physiognomy as a "present" that becomes ever more intense without empty exhibition, just like the "Amen" of his spirit before each unfolding of which he had presentiment and which he saw at every stage of the divine call.

His uncompromising conduct is well known. He loved his relatives with intense tenderness, but he made none of them rich or well off. His brother was not able to move to Rome; instead he continued in his modest employment. It was his will that his sisters, whom he had brought with him, be addressed and presented simply as "the Pope's sisters" and insisted that an automobile that had been given to them be sold. He opposed every promotion proposed for his nephew, Msgr. Parolin. He had a most tenacious memory and, even as Pope, he would welcome the humblest persons who came from his region. He would stay to speak with them in his beautiful Venetian dialect and his usual exterior majesty would seem to be replaced by the descent of a brighter one from heaven, which brought tears to the eyes of those speaking with him.

Due to the protocols of the pontifical court and its majesty, he was not always able to satisfy his desire to humble himself, but those who were closest to him witnessed the torment that ceremony caused him, and how he always sought to reduce the distance between himself and others as quickly as possible. For his own part, he had no personal needs. His *Summary of Virtues* is studded with pearls of great Franciscan joy. Even as Pope, he kept buttons, needles, and thread for making small repairs to his clothes. He brought Inchiostro, his cook from Venice, whose incompetence was a difficult test to the palate and digestion of the Pope's two secretaries, but not to that of the Pope, who was satisfied with everything. He forbade applause inside St. Peter's and would not allow his foot to be kissed. He participated personally in the spiritual exercises held in the Vatican, and seated himself among the public with the greatest naturalness. In a now-famous conversation that he had during the Conclave, Cardinal Mathieu asked him, "Do you speak French?" He replied, "Not at all, my lord." Cardinal Mathieu told him, "Then you are not eligible to be Pope." To which he rejoined, "Thanks be to God!"[a] Sometimes it was reported to him that his papal blessing, or contact with some personal object, had worked graces or healings. To such reports, he would reply with the unfailing aid of his superior sense of humor, "Ah, my dear, in this world we must be ready for anything!"[b] or, "Is it not strange that he has been healed by my waistcoat and I have not?"[c] His greatest suffering lay in not being able to give free rein to this intimate impulse of his heart at all times. He must have suffered immensely, particularly because he must have quickly become aware, as well—according to Don Orione—of "those petty influences that usually surround the powerful." He got rid of his guard. He got rid of the cupbearer and the escort from the Noble Guard that accompanied him on his afternoon stroll in the Vatican gardens. As much as possible, he eliminated the protocols, which caused him such immense discomfort.

Surrounded by the ineradicable pomp of the Roman See, which had built itself up over the centuries, he felt like a prisoner inside his soul almost more than inside his body. According to Msgr. Canali,[d] who sometimes filled in for an ailing Cardinal Merry del Val in daily relations,

---

[a] "Scis loqui gallice? – Nequàquam, Domine. – Ergo non es papabilis. – Deo gratias!"
Cf. François-Désiré Mathieu, *Les derniers jours de Léon XIII et le Conclave* (Paris: Librairie Victor Lecoffre, 1904), 71. Cf. Hieronymo Dal-Gal, *Pius X: The Life-Story of the Beatus*, trans. Thomas F. Murray (1953; repr., Dublin: M. H. Gill and Son, 1954), 134.

[b] Testimony of Msgr. L. Pisanello, cf. Girolamo Dal-Gal, *Il Papa Santo Pio X* (Padua: Il Messaggero di S. Antonio, 1954), 346.

[c] Cf. Dal-Gal, *Pius X Life-Story*, 213. Dal-Gal recounts a similar joke made by Pius X at a miracle attributed to the Pope's socks.

[d] Fabro's usage of the title "Monsignor" has been retained in this profile, even when referring to certain bishops or cardinals.

soon after he had risen to the pontifical throne, he was approached by a representative of the Italian government who wished to explore the political direction of the new Pope. The answer he gave was, "Tell the government that I do not wish to engage in politics!" His response to the most complicated affairs was, "I look upon the Crucifix!"[e] He had a passion for simplicity, but without affectation. Confronted by a vain person who made much of academic titles, he once burst out, "I know of a man who, without being a doctor of theology, became monsignor, bishop, cardinal, . . . and Pope!"[f] In similar fashion, his well-known courtesy toward Jews—especially toward Romanin-Jacur, the deputy who was the right arm of his charity at Mantua and in Venice—is expressed by the phrase: "In Mantua, my best Catholics are the Jews!"[g]

He was also simple in his very life of piety, which was deeply felt, but free from prolonged and superfluous routines that did not come from the majesty of the rite and interior recollection. Indeed, in the celebration of Holy Mass, he was averse to all eccentricities and throughout kept himself within the bounds of normalcy. Yet, his moving elocution and the holy candor of his face had a captivating and unforgettable impact on those who were present. He said the Rosary with the members of his household and often he recited the Breviary with his two secretaries, Msgr. Bressan and Msgr. Pescini. He would serve a second thanksgiving Mass for these secretaries when the chamberlain was not ready, as he had been accustomed to do for priests passing through Mantua or Venice, as had happened to Msgr. Ratti. This simplicity was present in his charity toward those suffering and troubled by misfortune, whom he treated as living members of his own body because they were members of the Mystical Body of Christ. It was known that he "preferred and loved the poor more than the rich," however, he advocated courtesy with both. In 1908, at the news of the earthquake, he planned to go to Messina and Reggio Calabria himself to bring his consolation. Using his excellent administrative ability, he personally oversaw the distribution of the most urgent and compassionate aid.

His guileless faith made him a sure judge of events and men, who was not subject to misdirection or backsliding. To Msgr. Pasetto, who had come to an audience before preaching the spiritual exercises, he made the firm recommendation: "Death, Judgment, Hell, and Heaven: these

---

[e] Cf. Dal-Gal, *Pius X Life-Story*, 173.
[f] Cf. Dal-Gal, *Pius X Life-Story*, 187.
[g] Cf. Emilio Zanzi, "Pio decimo," *La Stampa* (Turin), August 20, 1914, cited in Andrew M. Canepa, "Pius X and the Jews: A Reappraisal," *Church History* 61, no. 3 (September 1992): 366.

are the topics that the Pope and cardinals need." After the first sermon, he immediately congratulated the preacher: "Well done, Father. That's the way!" He was opposed to the idea of "career" and, when speaking with cardinals, he admonished them in a style reminiscent of St. Catherine of Siena: "Your purple will not save you from the judgment of God, unless it is honored by good works."

When the dominant Freemasonry confiscated all the possessions of the Portuguese bishops, he called Msgr. Pacelli, begging him to consider a relief proposal. The project entailed the then-staggering expenditure of a million [lire], but the Pope did not hesitate for a moment to aid his brethren in the Episcopate. The next day, a stranger coming from abroad left an offering of exactly a million [lire]. "See," Pius X commented, "as it goes out, so it comes in."[h]

Yet, there arose from the whole person of Pius X a mysterious sense of greatness that did not, however, erect false barriers of distance. The vast work of reform of the Church that he carried out with generosity and fortitude of spirit, because of the difficulty of the time and the urgency of the remedies, sets his Pontificate alongside and in the light of that of St. Pius V, who saved the faith of the Christian West from Islam. Pius X saved the Church from the conspiracy of all the heresies of modern culture, of politics, of the economy, those of historical and positive sciences, those of philosophy, and those of the new theology descending from beyond the Alps. An entire life dedicated to pastoral ministry in direct contact with souls in all the ranks of the hierarchy, as chaplain, pastor, bishop, and patriarch, gave him a knowledge of men from the most disparate conditions and revealed all the contingencies of human weaknesses and passions that, among these same Catholics, frequently interfere with the path of goodness. When he ascended the pontifical throne, the fact, too, that he had spent the greater part of his life away from all bureaucracy allowed him to work with a spirit of freedom that shook and troubled those who were loyal to the weight of tradition. We know that the most important act, which came from his independence of judgment, was the appointment of the young Msgr. Merry del Val, already Secretary of the Conclave, as Secretary of State. The greatness of his work in the spiritual regeneration of the Church emerges above all—and according to the express insistence of many of the witnesses at the Process—from the following provisions:

[h] Testimony of Msgr. Alberto Arborio Mella di Sant'Elia, cf. Dal-Gal, *Il Papa Santo*, 342 f.; *Pius X Life-Story*, 204.

The prohibition of a veto in the Conclave by any power, and the Constitution on the Conclave that he issued, which continue to regulate the election of his successors even now. However, as was demonstrated by the statistical evidence in the measured *Memoirs* of Cardinal Merry del Val, the election of Pius X was not at all the consequence of the veto of Franz Joseph brought by Cardinal Puzyna, because his candidacy was already secure when the veto was read.[i]

The codification of the Law of the Church—already desired by the Vatican Council—because of the morass of laws, which were a torment to the bishops who had to apply them and to enforce them. Pius X conceived the project soon after his election, chose the Commission, and set down the rules of the work in his own hand. During certain periods, he received almost every day the Secretary, Mons. Eugenio Pacelli, with whom he discussed point by point the work of the Commission, offering congratulations for the immense work, of which he was not able to see the completion. (His work is remembered in all its greatness by the Constitution *Providentissima Mater Ecclesia* of Benedict XV, who promulgated the new *Code of Canon Law* in 1917, and in the Preface by the President of the Commission, Cardinal Pietro Gasparri, which tells the story of the providential work).

The reform of Christian life. First are his specifications for the moral and intellectual formation of young clergy: We owe to him the idea to erect the first regional seminaries for the education of seminarians from dioceses which could not guarantee an adequate course of studies in the smaller diocesan seminaries. On August 4, 1908, the 50th anniversary of his priesthood, he published the admirable *Exhortatio ad Clerum*, which, as Cardinal Merry del Val attests, was written entirely in his own hand in little more than fifteen days, in bits of his spare time. With a practical spirit and in direct response to the attitude of the people, he reduced the large number of holy days of obligation to ten, with the specific intention of diminishing the sins to which modern dynamism and the relaxation of faith expose the faithful. On this matter, he was adamant. He responded to all the objections and protests by declaring himself willing to eliminate even the remaining feasts, and to move Christmas itself to Sunday as well, should it become apparent that the majority of the faithful would not observe it. He simplified and reordered the Breviary, making it shorter on Sundays and feast days, so that priests would have the necessary time

---

[i] Cf. Cardinal Merry Del Val, *Memories of Pope Pius X* (1939; repr., Westminster: Newman Press, 1956), 1 ff.

to attend to the sacred mysteries for the advantage of souls. He urged everyone, and especially bishops, to do their duty with a most generous immolation, and the speech that he made to the fourteen French bishops, whom he consecrated and sent to their respective dioceses, deprived of every benefice after the break with the government of France, remains memorable. Pius X is the Pope of the Catechism, the new draft of which he personally oversaw and which still remains in force. On Sunday afternoons, in the first years of his Pontificate, he explained the fundamental truths of the faith in a simple and easy style to the faithful of the parishes of Rome who gathered in the courtyard of St. Damasus: like a good shepherd renewing the presence of the Savior among the sheep of the divine sheepfold. A halo of angelic light and the fragrance of lilies linger around the Decree *Quam Singulari*, which announced the admission of children to First Communion as soon as they had reached the age of reason. He defended it often by affirming that "God must take possession of their innocent souls before they know evil and the devil enters into them!"[j]

Among his concerns as universal Pastor, the diocese of Rome always received his most vigilant solicitude. He reorganized the Vicariate, streamlining its structure in order to adapt it to the needs of the times. He sent ecclesiastics who did not have a specific assignment away from Rome, back to their respective dioceses. In the suburbs of Rome, he created a good number of new parishes and entrusted the care of souls in them to the religious.

He had a profound love for liturgical music. While in Venice, he replaced the Maestro di Cappella[k] with the young Lorenzo Perosi, whom he had directed to the priesthood. He later named Perosi as perpetual director of the Sistine Chapel. For the reform of sacred music, he founded the Pontifical Institute of Sacred Music in Rome, which has promoted, throughout the world, the advancement of an art form that owes its most original and most daring developments to the rich wealth of Christianity's dogmas. In the footsteps of Leo XIII, he worked hard for a return to the genuine doctrines of St. Thomas in seminaries and Catholic schools; as bishop, he explained his doctrine to the clergy of Mantua and Venice; as Pope, he wanted to have near himself theologians and philosophers of sure Thomistic orthodoxy.

---

[j] Cf. Dal-Gal, *Pius X Life-Story*, 183.
[k] Master of the Chapel, or choirmaster.

However, the greatest monument of his Pontificate and at the same time his personal cross was his condemnation of modernism. Even as bishop, he had perceived the deadly snares of this new heresy with the instinct of faith. From the pontifical throne, he intensified his research regarding the error that was spreading through both laity and clergy, creating confusion and sometimes exploiting even the good faith of those at the highest levels of the Church hierarchy. The struggle against modernism is perhaps the most personal work of Pius X and—although it may seem paradoxical—it is also the one that best reflects the stature and character of his spirit. After long years of research and study, he made his irreversible decision. On July 3, 1907, he released the Decree *Lamentabili*, the Syllabus against modernism that documented as many as 65 errors in the new teachings and touched upon all the vital points of the Catholic faith (Sacred Scripture, ecclesiastical Magisterium, divine revelation, the content of its dogmas and in particular those regarding the divinity of Jesus Christ, the nature of the sacraments, and the authority of the ecclesiastical Magisterium). In September of the same year, he issued the Encyclical *Pascendi*, which gave an irrefutable and logical synthesis of the modernist system and the charter to fight it in the heart of the Church. In order to avoid any ambiguity or compromise, regarding which the advocates of the new doctrine were indefatigable, the Pope issued the Motu Proprio *Sacrorum Antistitum* with the formula of the "oath against modernism" on September 1, 1910. Taking the oath became obligatory for assuming ecclesiastical offices and benefices, as well as for the conferring of academic degrees.

Considering its content, approach, and even its completely unmistakable style, *Pascendi* is one of the most decisive documents of the supreme Magisterium—indeed, as its most immediate offshoot, it is the most important after the Vatican Council, to which Christian life and Christian doctrine in the first half of the century owe their spiritual features and their salvation. Out of all the Acts of Pius X, it remains the most celebrated document of his Pontificate, the completion of that dyke against the tide of modern errors, which for a century had required the Roman Pontiff to labor in the defense of orthodoxy. Its strength lies in its solid theoretical structure, which lends it a persuasive force of singular clarity. According to Giovanni Gentile, this structure makes it "an authoritative exposition and a magnificent critique."[1] The Encyclical's

---

[1] Giovanni Gentile, "Il modernismo e l'enciclica," *La Critica* 6, no. 3 (May 1908): 213.

value is in having grouped together a disorderly avalanche of errors under the common term of "modernism" and then in having reduced them to their fundamental principles with ironclad logic. The errors previously denounced in the Decree *Lamentabili* are addressed again in the Encyclical in a way that reveals their real source and meaning, in order to unmask the deliberately vague manner in which their advocates presented them. In this sense, very soon after the Decree was issued, the way in which the Encyclical uses the adversary's terminology and technique to give a new and original exposition of already known errors is perhaps unique for a document of this sort. Therefore, it was suitable for the task of correcting those who, in good faith, might have been fighting on the side of error. The so-called *Programma dei Modernisti*[m] published in November 1907, as a reply to the Encyclical, accepts and even depends on the approach that the Encyclical had given to their doctrines. We know from the *Summary* that the Pope had had the first part of the Encyclical prepared with the help of three collaborators, one of whom was an authentic modernist (such an audacious move may be unique in the history of the Church). By identifying it in the most hidden corners, he cut off any means of escape for those who fostered error. The Pope was unwavering in taking remedial action against the recalcitrant and against those who wished to protect themselves behind the screen of ambiguity. Yet, he showed himself to be paternal by using every means possible to attract all those he saw to be moved by a sincere love of truth. Also well known is his personal defense of the orthodoxy of the great Cardinal Newman, whom modernist propaganda had been flaunting as one of their representatives.

To many, the Pope's forceful conduct against modernism seemed to border on injustice. They felt that he had been too hasty in accepting denunciations against even bishops and cardinals whose orthodoxy and fidelity to the Apostolic See ought to have been beyond reproach. The very fact that the *Summary* reports these complaints without reticence are evidence of the objectivity and integrity of the process instituted by the Church to examine the sanctity of her children, even those seated on its most august throne. These discordant judgments, some of which were expressed in the most drastic fashion, benefited his cause by deepening the knowledge of a holiness that consisted entirely in an absolute fidelity to that preservation of the faith which, just as it drives martyrs to a bloody

---

[m] *The Programme of Modernism* (London: T. Fisher Unwin, 1908).

sacrifice, so it is the support of the infallible Teacher in the most serious decisions. The most profound reason for the Pope's severity was the extreme horror that Pius X felt for heresy and the deadly anguish that he experienced in the face of the threat that modernism and its poison posed to the very wellspring of Christianity's fundamental truths or to those of any religion resting on transcendence. His figure rises up with the fierceness of the Apostolic Fathers who were compelled to combat the snares of Jewish and Hellenistic Gnosticism. Modernism is the Gnosticism of our times. It is the distillation of three centuries of philosophy determined to abolish the Absolute definitively and, having dissolved the anemic religiosity of Protestantism into the atheism of liberal theology, was preparing a coffin for Catholicism itself. In this fearful predicament, the equal of which the Church perhaps had not seen since Luther's rebellion, the Pope felt the threat of the storm in all its nefarious power like an invisible wound of interior heartache. We should not therefore be amazed if, in the middle of this stormy tempest, control of the rudder is given into the hands of one capable of making strong turns to save the barque from the treacherous rocks. In the decades that followed, events in the history of the Church have given him full witness. Struck at its heart, modernism immediately fell apart like a hollow shell and did not rise again, except sporadically. The rebels who remained obstinate became lost in their own vain ideas as they tore each other apart. The Church resumed its journey with new energy. Having been stimulated by the danger, the ecclesiastical sciences again flourished everywhere and, under the guidance of pontifical instructions, renewed their methods in accord with the resources of the most advanced scientific research in order to respond more adequately to the legitimate demands of the more mature modern conscience. If today, philosophy, theology, and the biblical and historical sciences have been reorganized according to their various facets in the pontifical faculties and in the seminaries without rash concessions or fearful restrictions, it is due especially to the cry of truth broadcast by *Pascendi*. This is why it remains the greatest claim to glory, both spiritual and human, of Pius X's Pontificate.

* * *

These bare hints regarding the work and person of the Pontiff remain immensely inadequate in conveying the reality. Immolated by his mission of universal paternity toward souls, the work and the soul of a Pope escapes into the mystery of his communion with God, and means of measuring it fails us. Yet, at the moment of lifting him to the altars, the Church that had him as her infallible Head allows us to consider him a little in his genuine physiognomy and permits him to come down into his actual existence, on this side of the schemes of life and mission of another time. At such a close distance, the figure of Pius X grows in greatness and splendor in the evidence of that sanctity which, in his case, was achieved at the high cost of struggle and renunciation. Beneath his apparent bonhomie, which has been avidly utilized by cheap literature for its easy apologetic or derogatory exploitation, Pope Sarto hid a complex and rich personality, tough as diamond, which disconcerted the shortsighted and fainthearted. The *Memoirs* of Cardinal Merry del Val allow for an unexpected glimpse of this personality, which is further illuminated by indicative references to other phases of his life.

It appears, therefore, that Pius X had by nature a fiery and sanguine temperament, which, at times, took the shocking forms of impulsiveness and indignation, especially during his early years of caring for souls. In Tombolo and Salzano, there are still some old men (as is noted already in the texts of the Process) who remember being dealt salutary slaps during catechism, which brought the more restless students immediately back on the right track. This firmness did not fail even in the face of the powerful, when he came across grave moral disorders. As bishop, cardinal, and even as Pope, he was never willing to receive those who who acted shamefully. A translucent soul, he did not tolerate duplicity from anyone, and if he became aware that someone had violated his trust, it was difficult for that person to regain his confidence. His judgment was like a sharpened sword that never missed its target. He never complained about the isolation in which he found himself at the most critical moments, and for which he was even blamed. He only expressed sorrow and protest when he saw the blows and attacks directed against his collaborators, especially Cardinal Merry del Val and Msgr. Canali, because he desired to reserve the bitter chalice entirely to himself.

Having given an example of complete subjection as chaplain, parish priest, bishop, and cardinal, he required absolute obedience from his own subjects, but in perfect loyalty. In Venice, he reproved Msgr. Apollonio, the archpriest of St. Mark, in the presence of the clergy, for having had the end of the Mass rung during the pontifical homily, against his specific instructions. Again, as Patriarch of Venice, he wrote a letter of complaint directly to the Pope—admirable for its vigor and pastoral sentiment—protesting the pontifical nomination, to an influential urban parish, of a candidate who had plotted to obtain support from powerful people.

Familiar as he was with this burning heart, Leo XIII, who was not at all offended, had the nomination annulled, and accepted instead the Patriarch's candidate, who completely fulfilled all his expectations. When, as Pope, he had grave decisions to make, he gave much time to prayer and reflection. Yet, when the moment for decision came, the firmness of his voice and personal attitude were such that no one would have dared to contradict him. It was an external irradiation of the theological virtue of faith drawn from its source. He even infused this faith into his collaborators, as Cardinal Merry del Val testifies, which resulted in a mixed impression of both trust and shock: the feeling that one has been propelled up to the threshold of the Absolute.

It might even be said without fear of error that this strength of faith was the characteristic virtue of his Pontificate. He placed his mission of universal Teacher of souls above everything and in its fulfillment, he would entertain no half measures or hesitations. He saw to the heart of things almost by instinct; he knew how to capture the "essence of a situation and then to propose solutions" with few words and without any frills or gimmicks. Just as he was able to generously overlook the miseries of human frailty, so too was he able to stand firm on questions of principle. If he met with opposition regarding any matter that he had studied in depth, he reacted with energy, raising his voice and slamming his fist on the table. Yet, at the same time, he also knew how to regain his composure quickly: his features resuming their habitually benevolent expression and his heart opening affectionately once he saw that his interlocutor had finally grasped the spirit and suffering of the Pope. He never held a grudge against his numerous and tenacious personal opponents, nor did he ever treat them badly; instead, he left each in his place, seeking more than once a calming of the spirits which, not rarely, even at the last moment and with great sorrow on his part, was denied to him. Like most heroic saints, he had powerful flaws, but, by his fighting them resolutely, they became the ladder to his sanctity.

The witnesses, especially those who were close to him as Pope, agree that, when he was meditating or praying, or just speaking of heavenly things, he conveyed the impression of something mysterious and heavenly in his person. Nevertheless, in private, his spirit yearned to expand in proportion to the exuberant cordiality that flowed from the living waters of joy welling up in his heart. We all know how concerned he was to avoid even the slightest trace of pretension or affectation, which so easily tempt the powerful into forgetting the true measure of their strength. As a true Christian Socrates, in the footsteps of St. Philip Neri, he knew how to find a witty way of denouncing the vanity of all finite things that revealed an unshakable trust in God. It is the explicit conviction of some of the witnesses, who knew him through long and intimate contact, that during his years in Rome his virtue fostered in him a profound transformation in holiness. With the passing of the years, in the course of fulfilling his highest mission, his sanctity became more and more evident. His exceptional commitment to the spiritual ascent confirms it. Unexpectedly and to his own deep dismay, he rose to the supreme Pontificate; yet, according to the *Summary*, he had actually predicted it to himself many years earlier, in the form of a joke, his usual way of speaking about himself.

From the height of the only seat of truth that God has placed on earth, Giuseppe Sarto, through the magnificence of his thought and the firmness of his purpose, renewed the face of the Bride of Christ, by taking upon himself all the trials, anxieties, and sorrows of her children. Robust in body, like an oak tree, even in old age, he declined rapidly under the sorrowful blows of the "Great War" of 1914, which he had foreseen as early as 1911, which broke out despite his most lively appeals and impassioned pleas. The dejecting vision of so many innocent children going to their massacre, because of the useless and criminal ambitions of the powerful, snuffed out his will to live, extinguishing him as a pure holocaust.

The "Letters" of St. Pius X

Men of action rarely commit to paper the intimate movements of their spirit, either because they are obliged by duty to contend with ever-changing circumstances or because they conduct the discourse of their life not with themselves, but with the world, with its obstacles, and with the goal toward which they are moving. However, when this action derives from a very high ideal of the good, there is an unfailing impulse toward reflection and the confidence in friendship that finds perfect expression in the letter. It serves as a beneficial pause in the tension of action, as well as a truthful mirror of the limit of one's strength for the task when compared without pretense against the measure of one's own ideal. Even then, it is not so much the letters left to us, fragmentary and intermittent as they are, which yield the person's authentic voice, but the quality of their purpose and the intensity of the commitment that forms the continuous thread and source of the energy unleashed in action. These are the reference points that may lend some continuity and effective substance to those occasional fragments and effusions. Even though it can furnish the most appealing fragments in the study of a personality, unless the letter is guided by the principle that inspired its writer's personality, it frequently runs the risk of creating ambiguity and dispersion.

Pius X did not want to be a writer and frequently joked about what he called his unfitness for poetry. As is perhaps typical for the very strong and action-oriented, his personality is still waiting to be understood and appreciated in a way befitting the accomplishments of an ecclesiastical "curriculum" that was possibly the one best suited to the offices in which he served, even more than for the very highest dignity that he reached through a humble, human itinerary filled with lively experiences and arduous battles, especially and specifically in light of the gradual ascent for which Providence was preparing him with great timeliness. Instructed in the harsh demands and spiritual beauties of poverty, Giuseppe Sarto always maintained frankness with himself and others. He was always alert to the fluctuations of human events around him in order to be able to judge them according to a sure criterion. As one who is not scandalized by evil because of his trusting confidence in the good, he could appreciate the work of others with detachment and at the same time with intimate participation. This first collection of his letters,[1a] which is offered to us with a rare editorial brilliance and the happy guide of precious historical and biographical details, opens a new window of understanding on the clear sky of the great soul of the Holy Pontiff. Still, these letters are unfortunately few in number and written to few correspondents, taking into account the vastness of his work and the abundance of encounters to which it must have given rise. However, even as they are, these letters of Pope Sarto often are a delightful document that is indispensable for putting him in the proper context within the concrete reality of the history of the Church in the last century.

The collection spans his whole life. The letters have been divided according to the main periods of his life, beginning with the entry of the fifteen-year-old youth into the Seminary of Padua and including the various charges and offices of his priestly life: chaplain, parish priest, chancellor of the Curia, bishop, cardinal, and Pope. If we desire to hear the profound echo of the soul that penned them, we should read these letters with attention, but without literary or diplomatic intent. Immediately obvious and perhaps disconcerting is the complete lack of any decidedly spiritual, ascetical, or mystical air, if you will, in the collection of St. Pius X's letters. These letters are concerned with urgent problems of life, concrete tasks and affairs; they are "business letters" (p. VIII). They testify to that characteristic of the man of action to which we have alluded. However, though the collection does not furnish us, insofar as I have been able to see, with a single example of what is considered spiritual direction in a strict sense, yet the collection itself is the eloquent evidence of a spiritual life in act, which rests on very solid

---

[1] St. Pius X, *Lettere*, collected by Nello Vian, Angelo Belardetti Editore, Rome 1954.

[a] Throughout the letters, Fabro italicized various words or phrases, either to emphasize or to indicate words in Latin or dialect. For most of the Latin phrases, the English translation has been given in brackets immediately following the Latin. Occasional exceptions have been made according to the editor's discretion.

and clear principles. Though these are often seen only indirectly, it is for this very reason that they become more compelling in the immediacy of a confidence or the urgency of responsibility.

Sometimes, they are only short notes. Very rarely are they elaborate letters, but either way, they are clear and unembellished. The only ones that engage in rhetoric, if we may call it that, are the very early letters of the young seminarian written to his cousin and namesake, Don Giuseppe Sarto, and to Don Pietro Jacuzzi, his chaplain in Riese, both of whom are the principal correspondents of this period. If one day he had had to reread those lines, a bit trite and clichéd, he would have been the first to smile at them. Admittedly, when this youth wrote, he always searched for the right word and wanted to give the best of himself. Of his entry into the seminary, he wrote: "I am sending you a few lines to inform you that, on the day of November 13, I entered the seminary; until this moment, I find myself well." At the end: "I flatter myself (!) that you enjoy perfect health" (*Lett.* 1). He continues the phrase "until this moment," adding "with all my companions and superiors and especially with the Professor (Don Evangelista De Piero, from Monselice) who is very good" (*Lett.* 2). In the second letter to his cousin, written when his cousin was approaching his priestly ordination, he informed him that the outcome of his term exams had been "sufficiently good." In reality, his marks, as would be the case throughout all his priestly studies, were the very best, as noted by the qualification: *In discipline second to none, of the greatest ability, (blest) with a very great memory, and (giving) the highest promise.*[2b] He assures him that his own health had gone "from good to better" and promises "that in the future my poor writings will be more frequent" (*Lett.* 3). The most emotional and vivid of these letters is the one written to his cousin when his cousin's mother died, very close to the date of his priestly ordination:

> And first of all, I trust you believe that from the moment I learned of the death of your beloved mother, your image has revolved in my mind as I pondered whether I could come up with something to bring some relief to your tears and suffering, but my own afflicted spirit

---

[2] On the "curriculum" of Sarto the seminarian, see: D. Ireneo Daniele, *La formazione di San Pio X nel Seminario di Padova*, in "Studia Patavina," I, 2 (1954), p. 286 ff.

[b] *Disciplinae nemini secundus, ingenii maximi, memoriae summae, spei maximae.*
English trans. from Hieronymo Dal-Gal, *Pius X: The Life-Story of the Beatus*, trans. Thomas F. Murray (1953; repr., Dublin: M. H. Gill and Son, 1954), 8.

did not allow it. But now that such a beautiful occasion has presented itself [your ordination], I trust that my words will joyfully wing their way to console you and to attest to the dear remembrance of you that I keep and will keep forever as the most beloved of my relations.

Since you will soon go up to the altar of the Most High and see your dear relatives around you, do not be grieved not to see your beloved mother among them. Find greater consolation that she is above in Paradise to welcome your prayers and to present them, united to her own, at the throne of the Supreme Giver of every good thing, in order that they be granted more easily.

In pledge of my gratitude and affection, I am sending you the attached epigram and I ask that you give it at least a glance, even though it is only a little thing not worthy of you, issued as it is from my poor intellect. (*Lett.* 5)

An enjoyable, early document depicting the frankness of spirit that characterized his whole life is a letter dated June 27, 1853 to Don Jacuzzi—"this genial, devout, and strong Friulano,"[c] as Dr. Vian refers to him. In it, he informs the new parochial vicar of his hometown about a prank at the seminary, which even a century later still conveys amiable simplicity and reveals, though implicitly, the writer's opinion of it:

Last Sunday, the nineteenth of the current month, while we were all at supper in the refectory, a loud jeer was directed at the second vice rector, who happened to be present for the beautiful compliment. You can now imagine the effects, which are experienced only by the dormitory to which I belong, since it was the first to commit such a deed. Meanwhile, the prefects, who refused to report any of the guilty persons, were all immediately dismissed from office, and some of them were punished. Two youths were very nearly dismissed from the seminary because a third, a most worthy person, took it upon himself to go and turn them in to the superiors. Nevertheless, they were spared such a great chastisement after they begged for mercy and expressed repentance. Many were then punished with a day in their room with the proper discipline, nor has this *old story* concluded yet. Amid all this confusion, even the innocent, among whom, thank Heaven, I can count myself, suffer something; meanwhile, greater rigor in discipline, and the rest that you can imagine. Enough! There is nothing for it but patience. (*Lett.* 9)

---

[c] Cf. Nello Vian, in *Lettere*, ix.

The joyfulness of his resigned and optimistic spirit does not abandon him even in the middle of the summer, when he writes again to Don Pietro, in the middle of July in the same 1853:

> The ninth of the present month will be the last day of the school year. On that same day, we will all leave the seminary, but, and here is the hard part, we must first undergo, and with rigorousness, the final exams. I am oppressed by the heat and tormented by mosquitoes, which cause me fatigue, the bitterest enemy of that study to which I must now principally apply myself. Still, I am rather well and take much comfort in the hope that I will soon be finished and will soon be able to see you again and enjoy your dear and welcome company.
>
> I will not go on at length. I beg you, give the enclosed to my mother, and my regards to my friends, while I desire for you as much consolation as you yearn for, embrace you from my heart, and declare myself for always [etc.]. (*Lett.* 10)

Unfortunately, the summer companionship of Don Pietro would end that year, with his transfer to Vascon.[d] He was replaced at Riese by a certain Don Pietro Pamio[e] whose attitude and habits it seems were very different from those of his predecessor, even in the perception of the people. Hence the young seminarian's discomfort, which he expresses to Don Jacuzzi without reserve, wishing to be able to return quickly to the seminary:

> As the poet says, it is a bitter thing to remember a happy time in the midst of misery. Yet, the other day, reading your kind and always welcome letter, I felt some delight in remembering the beautiful days spent in your company. Now it has all vanished. What is the point of birding these days, if the principal purpose is lacking? Singing attracts me little in the absence of that dear director and companion, who was for me my first comfort. As for the rectory, it is a place of solitude, and those who live in it, rather than consecrating a few hours to friendship, prefer instead to make their little excursions each day, and so I am almost always at home, cut off from everyone. Sometimes, I go to visit some friendly family, but caution is needful everywhere because, whenever I am seen, they begin to thunder speeches regarding this blessed archpriest which, to tell the truth, is a truly singular thing. Do you see, Don Pietro, what a wonderful fall

---

[d] "Varcon" in *Profili di Santi*.
[e] "Marmio" in *Profili di Santi*.

> I have in store? I am here wishing to return to the seminary to spend more tranquil days with a few books in the peace of my little room. (*Lett.* 11)

By now, the young seminarian had become mature enough to take an interest in and to play a direct role in improving the spiritual situation of his hometown. To his constant confidant, Don Pietro, now the chaplain in Cusignano, he writes:

> The Holy Exercises were finished yesterday and, during the 15 days since I returned to the seminary, I have put in order all that I had to do. Now, before I become involved in other things, I want to fulfill an obligation and a duty. Good as you are, you will have forgiven our lack of communication because, after so many promises, we have disappointed you, similar in these to those whom the poet described in that saying, *parturiunt montes nascetur ridiculus mus* [the mountains would go into labor and give birth to a ridiculous mouse].[f] To tell the truth, it looked as if all misfortune had conspired against the beautiful projects that we had made with Antonio. One time, he was busy; another time, a horse could not be found anywhere in Riese, and then, when we had found one, Toni was afflicted by such a headache that he did not know where he was. Finally, on the day when you had kindly offered me means of transportation with your dearest brother Leonardo, so as to cause no offense to the archpriest, I had joined a commission for a new chaplain, which in such severe circumstances, the parishioners demand. They have obtained nothing yet, and I believe that they will obtain nothing in the future either, because the so-called *Prelate* enjoys very little influence with Msgr. Farina[g] and with the others in the Curia, and meanwhile who pays the cost? The poor, little sheep, as the famous Dal Mistro used to say. Indeed, fortune has conspired against us. Let us hope that we shall be able to do next year what we have not done this year and, as they say, in order to avoid being cheated by time, we shall come at the beginning of the birding season rather than at its end and enjoy your beloved company. (*Lett.* 13)

Significant is the allusion that follows regarding the "new discipline" and his delight at having been exempted from it by the superiors:

---

[f] Horace, *Ars Poetica* 139.
[g] Fabro's usage of the title "Monsignor" has been retained in this profile, even when referring to certain bishops or cardinals.

Here at the seminary, I have spent six years well; I hope to spend this year even better than I have spent the others despite the new discipline that has been introduced. The good superiors, agreeing with my requests, after four years of service as prefect, have put me at rest, but *pede libero*.[h] Without the trouble, I still enjoy all the privileges; they have assigned to me a little room separate from the common, where one hears nothing other than the little bell and the clock. *Quid melius?* [What could be better?] On our walks, I will no longer have to go with those long lines that cause melancholy to those who see them and even more to those who form them. I will go with a good schoolmate, who is a friend. Again, I could not hope for better. In all tranquility, I look after my obligations, and so I hope to have some little time to respond to the desires of good friends with letters. See from this whether I can be happy. In this way, little by little, I begin to prepare for when I will be a chaplain, so that I will not find a life of solitude and study boring. Here the superiors call me the retiree, and have every good reason for doing so, and even if they should place some obligation on me, I will accept it willingly in response to such great goodness on their part. (*Lett.* 13)

Apart from showing his solid, habitual realism, the two letters to Don Jacuzzi and to his namesake cousin, which immediately precede his ordination to the major orders, offer nothing special (*Lett.* 14–15). He asks his cousin to pay the tax to the Curia to grant a dispensation due to age "because you already know my circumstances; without having made a vow of poverty, I find myself without money" (*Lett.* 15). Needless to say, the theme of poverty and financial worries recurs frequently in the letters. As the dynamic chaplain of Tombolo and archpriest of Salzano, he quickly burned through whatever little money he had, and he borrowed a great deal to finance the many charitable projects he initiated for the good of his flock. So it was that when he was promoted to Chancellor of the Curia of Treviso, the people of Salzano good-naturedly described him: *He came in garments that were torn, / He left without a shirt* (p. 54).[i]

---

[h] "*Pede libero*," in Horace, *Odes* I.37, 1: "Nunc est bibendum, nunc *pede libero*" [Now we must drink, and stamp the ground with a free foot].

[i] *El xe vegnùo co la veste sbrisa / El xe partio senza camisa.*
    English trans. from Igino Giordani, *Pius X: A Country Priest*, trans. Thomas J. Tobin (Milwaukee: Bruce Publishing Company, 1954), 29.

As he is launched into the high ecclesiastical life, his correspondence becomes more rigorous and reserved in its expression, manifesting the maturity of a man equal to his ability and with an extremely expert knowledge of individual psychology. Begged by his namesake cousin to help him to seek the restitution of a loan which the cousin had made to a certain Don Giovanni Rossi, archpriest of Treviso, the poor mediator did not find the task easy. He felt like he was caught between a rock and a hard place:

> I have seen Archpriest Rossi. As you must know, about a month ago, I had to go to his house regarding a certain dispute. He went on such a jeremiad about his own circumstances and of the harsh impossibility of satisfying the commitments in which he finds himself that I had to plan the second interview arranged after your recommendations so that I might again return to the charge. I have told him, then, of the letter that you have written to me, of your need to use what you lent to him, of your circumstances. With kind manners, I tried to persuade him to pay his debt. He resumed his jeremiads and laid out for me the long list of his debts, but we finally agreed that he will do all he can to cancel his debt. I wished him to give me a date, and a close one, but I was able to obtain no more than this word: that we will see each other in a few days, and then he will be able to give me a definitive answer. After all this, dear cousin, I must tell you that Pastor Rossi is in a sea of trouble and debts, and we shall be lucky if we succeed in getting him to repay you even a little at a time. In any case, I will write to you again with more details.
>
> In your letter, you wrote I have failed to keep my word. I am not surprised, as my memory sometimes fails me, and sometimes I lack the power to make a good impression on anyone even with goodwill, especially on you, toward whom I admit that I have failed and so confess my fault for more than once not having fulfilled my promises. If those words of your letter refer to the past, I hereby cry, *mea culpa, mea maxima culpa* [my fault, my most grievous fault], and implore a plenary indulgence. However, if they refer to a something more recent, do me the favor of writing me a line so that I may apply a remedy and, as is just, do the necessary penance. Do not believe that I am saying this in order to get back at you, or because I am offended by what you have written, but truly so that I may remedy my fault, if there is still time. (*Lett.* 41)

Yet the Reverend Cousin seems not to have been completely satisfied if his cousin, Monsignor the Chancellor, took up his pen to calm the storm once more:

> I have read your dear letter, and you have not one, but a thousand reasons to say and repeat that I am not only one *who fails to keep his word*, but also a wonderful buffoon. What can I say? Amid the confusion of a thousand cares, I truly forgot the promise I had made; in any case, this too is an evil that can be remedied. (*Lett.* 42)

During his stay in Treviso, he was delegated, along with Msgr. Saccol and others, to represent the Chapter of the Treviso Cathedral at the celebrations in Rome commemorating the 50th anniversary of the Episcopate of Pius IX.[3] The letters referring to it show the provincial prelate's habitual character of immediacy, and the humble but strong spirit of one who knows how to describe the incomparable greatness of the Holy City:

> Here, foreigners are respected by all, and it is enough to step into this blessed city to become aware that it is the exclusive City of the Popes. *Wonderful things* are told of the gifts presented to the Holy Father. In foreigners, as much as in citizens, a holy enthusiasm is tied to a most religious calm. I have only one fear; that of not being able to see the Holy Father, since the reception on day 4 was cancelled. I am very much afraid that Sunday, with such a great crowd, it will be difficult for us to be able to see him. (*Lett.* 45)

He was completely seized by the celebratory events and a legitimate desire to see the sacred monuments of Rome. In a second letter sent to his secretary, Msgr. Mander of Treviso, he is as ready as always to note the contrasting, and even slightly comic aspects of the situation. Writing in a rapid style, he recounts:

Yesterday's celebration was magnificent and all the more beautiful for the contrast. The session on Saturday evening, in preparation for the pilgrimage, was wonderful. There was an eloquent speech by the president of the Circle of Catholic Youth; the speech of a bishop of Etruria was also most beautiful, and Msgr. Parocchi's discourse was unimaginable.

---

[3] On this first visit to Rome, see Nello Vian, *Primo incontro con Roma di Giuseppe Sarto*, in "La Strenna dei romanisti," XV (1954).

> As His Eminence Cardinal Davanzo was making his own speech on Saturday night in front of St. Peter in Chains, he fainted and was carried away from the pulpit by four brawny priests. I have visited the holy monuments of Rome, but I am still just beginning, though I have been tireless and have not taken even an hour's rest. It is moving to encounter foreign pilgrims everywhere as they go to visit the churches and pray in such a way as to convey their own desire to even the most reticent and their fervor to even the most lukewarm. (*Lett.* 47)

Perhaps his most delicate letter, pervaded as it is by a deeply human tone, is the third one to the same Monsignor, who was serving as Secretary to the Bishop during the bishop's vacation.[j] It was written following a visit with Monsignor Vicar to a certain Archpriest Trevisi, who had been retired too hastily. The very beautiful letter opens in a joking tone:

> *Laus Deo* [Praise God], and let us begin the correspondence of letters for the vacation of 1878. If we were to sing of great things, it would be fitting, like the poets, to trouble Olympus. But having to scribble out four lines *tenui vel gracili avena* [with a weak or slender reed], we shall be satisfied with offering a greeting to the protector of the Curia, *quocumque se nomine vocet* [by whatever name he may call himself], and then, like preachers, we shall say: *Incomincio* [I begin]. (*Lett.* 52)

A quick recounting of the daily work then followed:

> And I begin *in primis* [first] by apologizing for having allowed the first day to go by *sine linea* [without a line]. It is easy, of course, to guess the reason: I would not have known how to smear the little sheet of paper. Furthermore, let us understand each other from now on, and once and for all, let the proverb, no news is very good news, be our motto. A lack of letters, then, will signify that the *old Curia*, being as unresponsive to gentle manners as it is to harsh blows, according to its ancient custom, with the usual *tran-tran* [humdrum], continues to trot or walk in its usual groove. The same will be thought here of those who are far away. Has no news come? A good sign. "Now they have risen and breathe the balmy airs of the hills; now

---

[j] Msgr. Mander accompanied the bishop during his time of rest in Montebelluna.

they stand at their window contemplating the views of the hill and of the plain." In a little while, "they receive a visit, and then they breakfast. His Excellency is thoughtful because, although it is eight in the morning, he has not yet said *None*.[k] Mrs. Lisa reads the calendar, but she does not know how to find the antiphons. And then it is lunch time and there is a coach ride!" (*Lett.* 52)

But this is no more than a prologue in order to make known the deep suffering of the old ex-Archpriest Trevisi that the higher-ups might think about it and consider a solution:

> *A propos*, I change topic, otherwise those who say that in the Curia we waste time, we joke, and business is forgotten would not be wrong.
>
> Last night, with Monsignor Vicar, I went to visit Trevisi, who has begun to move on his own with the help of a little cane. He celebrated our arrival festively and assailed us with questions on the health of His Excellency, on the good and bad news of the diocese. He took some delight in the honor granted to Bonaventura and to the parish during the celebration, and in response to certain observations, he added quietly: "Remember that we are all human, and we need to hear some word from those on high. Such a word gives us joy or, if we are troubled, it consoles us." After this, there was silence for a while. I did not ask Monsignor Vicar what impression Trevisi's observations had made on him. Afterwards, I thought that since his resignation, (a day on which he received many attentions from the Bishop, regarding which he later wrote me to thank the Bishop for such kindness, a kindness of which even yesterday I was reminded) aside from communicating to him the announcement of the competition and then the appointment of the new archpriest, the Curia has had nothing more to do with poor Trevisi. Would it not be opportune, taking advantage of the installation (truly, it is a bit late, but better late than never), for the Bishop to issue a decree to him *de bono Parochiarum regimine* [on the good governance of parishes], confirming thus his titles of archpriest, abbot, and pro-vicar? If you think it good to speak of it to His Excellency, I am certain that Trevisi would not behave like certain fussy persons, and would, in fact, show his gratitude toward the Bishop for this too. (*Lett.* 52).

---

[k] The Ninth Hour of the Divine Office.

Having completed the charitable interlude, the letter resumes its joyful tone describing the enjoyable portrait of two old ladies, the Bishop's sisters, intent at their interminable prayers:

> Now I go upstairs to have news of the ladies.
> They are very well. Mrs. Bettina is hearing the last Mass in the cathedral, and I imagine that the good Mrs. Elena, as usual, is reciting her prayers. They are also well at home; this morning, I greeted Mrs. Augusta, who had opened the windows as early as possible. Kiss His Excellency's hand for me. (*Lett.* 52).

To this period of the Treviso Chancellorship belongs a long letter to his "dearest cousin," his namesake, wherein for the first time we read a biting observation regarding the emptiness and bitterness that human honors have in store for those who seek after them:

> For my part, you are not only my cousin, but also a dearest friend. Therefore, say clearly to whomever should talk to you that I know myself to be sufficiently small as not to aspire to those places. However, even if I should be called to them, I have beautiful examples to imitate in Panella, or Tessarin, nor would I hesitate for a moment to place myself in their ranks. A certain amount of experience acquired during five years in the Curia has made me aware of the thorns, the dangers, the responsibilities inherent in those places which are not equal to the paltry, tiny *glory* of a pastoral staff since this fades away, when we think about the fact of St. Philip. And then? And then? *And then, death.* (*Lett.* 54)

The rest of the letters, that is, the greater part of the present collection, refers to the subsequent periods in the high offices of Bishop of Mantua, Patriarch of Venice, and Sovereign Pontiff. To the previously known correspondents, numerous new ones are added due to the necessities of the high office. For the most part, they are official and governmental letters, which, in their brevity, are a model of pastoral governance. Ranking first is the one to Msgr. Giuseppe Callegari, bishop and later cardinal of Padua, to whom he first pours out the anguish of his heart because of his elevation to the Episcopate:

> To you before anyone else, I feel the duty, but also the need, to manifest the distress in which my poor spirit finds itself, because from you I await a word that may comfort me. After 15 days of painful agony, in the course of which I have thought of Your Excel-

lency a hundred times; a hundred times, I would have liked to find refuge in your embrace, but always I held myself in check with the expectation that I would bring you much happier news. However, yesterday the absolute confirmation reached me that the Holy Father wishes me to be bishop at Mantua. I have prayed, I have begged the Holy Father fervently that he would leave me, miserable as I am, in my poverty, but my prayers have not been granted. My dear Monsignor! I am to be bishop and in the diocese of Mantua, as successor to such learned and holy bishops as Msgr. Rota and Msgr. Berengo. Ah, pray for me to the good God that he may pour some balm on this wound and give me strength to carry the cross. (*Lett.* 80)

After his episcopal consecration, he addressed his first letter from Rome to the same bishop of Padua, on November 20, 1884. In it, he expresses the legitimate emotion caused by the event, which in no way quashes his holy realism in the midst of a world of empty flatteries, even when they are not all and not always insincere:

> Now we come to the visits, and these are a very great bother, because it is so difficult to find those whom we desire, whereas others make for a waste of time for their possible ineffectiveness. To what an awful condition I have been reduced! I cannot yet tell you when I will leave Rome, because there are still too many things to be started, and furthermore my days fly like thunderbolts that are finished before they are barely started.
>
> Continue to pray for this poor honest man, who begs you to express his reverence ever so much to Mother and Aunt; greet everyone for me and, because you give me so much confidence, I send you a kiss from the heart. (*Lett.* 82)

The lament of the "poor honest man" is repeated with greater desolation in the letter dated December 3, in which he expresses gratitude and seeks some comfort from his brother bishop:

> After four days, it is surely time to surface again before you to fulfill the duty of thanking you for the new proofs of affection which you have been pleased to give me. Yet I have a head that is so broken; I do not know which way to turn. Visits morning, evening, and at all hours—letters raining in from Mantua, even some curious ones, that require considered responses. In conclusion, if some saint does not provide, I will not last. (*Lett.* 83)

Now, it is through the letters that we should follow the complex pastoral activity of this zealous bishop, now part of history. They ought to be studied on their own and placed within the context of events, particularly those addressed to ecclesiastical and civil authorities. Instead, let us glean some things from the lesser letters. There are his condolences to the Commendatore Re, his procurator at the Roman Curia, on the death of his daughter, little Adelaide Re:

> Oh poor Peppino and poor Mrs. Re! I do not have the courage to say, poor Adelaide, because this little angel looks upon her dear ones from Paradise and from there prays for holy resignation for her father and mother. I invoke the same with my whole soul because only in it can they find some respite. Oh, how quickly the holy joys of the family are changed into mourning and the sweetest of affections, as they are the cause of ineffable joy, so they are unfortunately the cause of unspeakable bitterness! Sharing in a most lively way in the sorrow of all, I make repeated prayer that God may heed the vast emptiness left in your heart and may console all of you by healing your wound. (*Lett.* 89)

He does not forget simple cordiality with his old friends. He apologizes to Msgr. Giovanni Milanese, of the Seminary of Treviso, for corresponding so rarely:

> Neither scruples nor regrets are sufficient any longer to bring about a man's reform. The *I cannot*, which so often is a pretext, has for me become a real obstacle; with all goodwill, I am not sufficient for everybody and everything. But I do not wish it to be said that I have forgotten you, and so this morning, before the visitors arrive, I want to write at least a line to thank you for your dear letter which you have had delivered to me through the very good Countess Emma. Through the foolishness of my Beppo,[1] who does not yet know how to distinguish between white and red, I did not have the pleasure of offering her my regards before her return to Treviso. I hope that she will have received my note and will have presented my apologies to you and to her family. As for you, do add all that in which I may have failed, and say it clearly, because I will not take offense, because it is a miracle that I do not lose my head. (*Lett.* 91)

---

[1] Nickname for Giuseppe.

Yet his spirit continued to be always keen and his judgment of men firmly realistic:

> Things proceed pretty well here, but one must never become sleepy because everyone else is too awake and, out of concern that the Bishop's health may suffer, they are always ready to take on any office, even if it were not to be offered to them directly. Therefore, I do not know whether I will always be able to stand on my own feet amid the thousand difficulties that I encounter on my way. In any case, let us move forward and put our trust in Providence. (*Lett.* 91)

Toward the end, he pens an amiable little note:

> Say to Paronetto (a canon of Treviso) that I thank him dearly for his letter, to which I will reply soon. Many thanks to Don Francesco for his dear remembrance. Tell him that sometimes I dream that I hear his voice: *Monsignor! What time is it?* (*Lett.* 91)

His congratulations sent to Msgr. G. Milanese for the promotion of "Don Checco" (probably Don Francesco Zanotto) to canon, read enjoyably:

> Give my greetings to all and tell our friend Don Checco that I hope, with the venerable signs of his canonry, that he will forget that he is young and take on such gravity as is suitable for a canon. He can take lessons in gravity from one who, as his senior, is in a position to teach it. Poor Belgium! And poor philiology! Caught in those *thickets*! It is fortunate that he will find asylum in the College of Cantarane. There, he will move all those still simple souls of St. Teresa (apart from one) with his tears. (*Lett.* 99)

Likewise, this hint of irony, with personal experience, is sent to Don Agnoletti:

> I am pleased that your Lenten preaching finished with applause and an abundant draft of large *sturgeons*. Nevertheless, I recommend that you not make too many visits to those hills. I have a good memory and remember some return trips from those towns made in a truly happy state, if not a very stable one: my legs did not wish to obey my head, or my head asked the impossible from my legs. *Caute negotiare* [Move cautiously]. At fifty, one must not move with too much confidence. Excuse me if I am preaching to you, but we are on the topic, since we were speaking of Lenten preaching. (*Lett.* 153)

The letter sent to Don Olivo Luisetto, secretary to Msgr. Callegari, who was then recovering from a grave illness, to recommend to the latter the rigorous observance of the medical instructions, is a small masterpiece of affectionate care:

> As soon as I received your last letter with its brighter news about the regular course of the illness and the approaching, if perhaps not yet begun convalescence, and after giving thanks to the Lord, the moment seemed opportune to present His Excellency with my sincere congratulations and to preach a salutary sermon to him, not *ad correctionem* (entirely useless), but *ad praecautionem* (*date veniam verbo non satis latino*).^m To this end, I had already prepared a nice sheet of paper and was writing the relative passage. However, while the arguments *ad hominem* were flowing nicely, the terrible thought occurred to me, *quos ego* [What about me?]. Then I was seized by the fear of hearing repeated, with a severe look: from what pulpits do these sermons come? So, I tore up the paper and decided to write to you instead and beg you as a good secretary that, at the hour when you find our poor patient calmer, just to tell him this: A friend of his, who loves him dearly, an advocate for all those who desire to see you well and prosperous for many years, begs you to attend scrupulously to the instructions of the physician, remaining in total rest, and taking all possible care. See that you present my prayer to him in such a way that I may not at any time have to accept a rebuke, and affectionately kiss his hand for me. (*Lett.* 152)

A brief mention regarding the few letters to the Perosi family: The first, dated May 1884, is written to the father, Maestro Giuseppe in Tortona, from Mantua, where, already a cardinal, he was waiting to make his entry to Venice. He wrote to the father to thank him for having encouraged his son, Lorenzo, to accept the position of First Maestro in the celebrated Chapel of St. Mark:

> Be assured that not only will Lorenzino fulfill the expectations of the Venetians, but he will soon be welcomed by all with affection. At whatever time the Lord wants me in Venice, I will be an affectionate friend to him rather than a father. Meanwhile I offer to you my greatest congratulations on this good son of yours, who truly does

---

^m ... not *for correction* (entirely useless), but *as a precaution* (*grant indulgence for the word not being sufficiently Latin*).

honor to his family by the particular talents with which he is furnished, but much more for the beautiful virtues that render his genius wonderful. (*Lett.* 155)

Thus Lorenzino, the new genius of sacred music, was discovered and assisted by the Bishop who, as a seminarian and as a young priest in rural parishes, strove to restore and cultivate the ancient, nearly forgotten chant of the Church. Two other letters are directed to Lorenzo's brother, Don Carlo (who died a cardinal). The first expresses enthusiasm for the triumph gained by the oratorio *The Transfiguration*, performed for the first time in Venice for the occasion of the International Art Exposition in 1898:

> I am returning now from the Hall where Don Renzo's new oratorio was performed. The very large hall was entirely full of respectable and very intelligent persons. The very splendid performance exceeded expectations, which were in any case very great. Don Renzo was a little tired, but he was well, in part because he was now free of the worry, which oppressed him for the past few days. The first President of the Court of Appeal (the ex-minister Santamaria Nicolini) said to me, "Oh, this is an eloquent sermon! By the end, many were moved." (*Lett.* 197)

A second more demanding letter charges the prudent brother to guide Lorenzo in steering his way in the delicate position of Adjunct Director of the Sistine Chapel:

> I truly rejoiced in the Lord when Don Lorenzo wrote to me from Rome that he had declined the direction of the Mass for the canonization in favor of Mustafà.[4] The sacrifice he made in that letter to His Excellency the Majordomo surely will not be without great comfort. Furthermore, things had reached the point (I have been able to ascertain this by listening to all the parties) that such a sacrifice was absolutely necessary, in order that all who love and have been kind to Don Lorenzo not be exposed to grave displeasure, and that he not be compromised by the performance's lack of success, which was foreseen. In order to exact payback, it will be necessary for Don Lorenzo to remain silent and to proceed slowly for a while because his adversaries are many and powerful. Those above would like a peaceful agreement between the two directors, which is an

---

[4] The Master Director of the Sistine Chapel, whom, in a short while, Perosi would succeed.

absolute impossibility since principles are at stake. Hence, it will be necessary to gain ground bit by bit, until even the blind open their eyes and become convinced that they have not seen aright. I am not surprised at Cardinal M. for having said that they should make a fresh start, but it is one thing to say it and another to do it, and even though he too is a good friend to Don Renzo, yet arguments that convince do not always persuade. (*Lett.* 209)

Only two letters to Don Lorenzo himself are preserved here. The first, from 1885,[n] is addressed to Solesmes, from where the young priest had told him about the mystical enthusiasm that he had felt while listening to the chant of those monks. The letter is almost prophetic regarding the reform of Gregorian chant that he would carry out as Pope:

> I am truly grateful to you for remembering me and I rejoice in my soul that you have completed the first stage of your voyage safe and sound. With the simple announcement of the Vespers that you heard sung by those venerable monks, you have caused to grow in me the desire to hear the Lord praised in similar manner in Italy. It will be a long road, but I hope I do not die before I hear it. According to a note I read in the newspapers, it would appear that the Holy Father has already handed the new Regulations for Music, which will be printed shortly, to the Cardinal Prefect of the Congregation of Rites. Let us hope that all will be in conformity with our desires. (*Lett.* 159)

The second (*Lett.* 212) is a note of congratulations on the success of the oratorio, "The Massacre of the Innocents," at its first Roman performance in 1900.

* * *

Accustomed as he was to seeing life and its commitments with unconditional dedication, he applied the same personal vigilance and responsibility to whatever he did, whether it was great or small. Hence, as Cardinal Patriarch, he asks Agostino Vian, father of the industrious compiler of this volume, to "warn the Commission of Conferences that, as it publishes new announcements, it remember to bring a copy to the police headquarters, with all copies having been subjected to the stamp tax. There may be some who believe that this is not necessary, but you

---

[n] Rather, 1894

will do me the favor of telling him to thank the Lord that he has not paid a fine this time, and it is very practical for us not to make enemies" (*Lett.* 204). After he had been raised to the Pontificate, he sent a note of encouragement to the same correspondent, who had been a dear collaborator in his social works, to console him for not having succeeded in a competition for a job: "Do not become disheartened over this, for Providence will set aside for you another office, perhaps one better paid, and, if the opportunity arises, I will not fail to be of help to you" (*Lett.* 255). Then he adds wishes for the upcoming name day of the correspondent: "Meanwhile, I send in advance my wishes on your upcoming name day and with all my heart I impart the Apostolic Blessing on you, on Giuseppina, and on all your dear ones, with the desire that this be for each of you the source of sweetest consolations. Pius PP. X" (*Lett.* 255). Coming as it did from the memory of past struggles, the humility of writing in the first person singular must have transfigured the glad correspondents with purest joy. Let this suffice to give a little taste of the riches contained in this volume.

I leave the volume to the attentive reader. And these letters deserve very many readers, not only because of their high spiritual and historical value, but also and especially because of the atmosphere of deep and frank humanity that they breathe throughout. Nevertheless, one in particular merits to be quoted in its entirety. It is the only letter of spiritual direction I have found. It is addressed "To the good daughter Emilia Falavigna" in the Monastery of the Visitation of Verona. In it, we find the intimate spirit of the priest he must have been, full of tenderness and flights of bliss, when he was in direct contact with souls called to the life of perfection. The brief letter is sent from Mantua on October 14, 1886:

> I received true comfort from your letter, in which you share that the Lord is pleased to give you joy in your life of retirement with his holiest consolations. I desire with my whole heart that the divine Jesus ever show himself to you as your sweetest brother and friend. However, do not let this tranquility make you certain that he may not at times also prepare some mortifications for you. This sweetest Spouse often rejoices in visiting those souls that are dear to him with crosses. You must prepare yourself to run this course as well with much courage, considering that the road to Paradise is not always to be found amid sweet things and flowers, but amid thorns and stones. As you aspire to form your heart in the image of the Most Sacred Heart of Jesus, you must be ready to carry the cross with Jesus

and to go up to Calvary with him. Do not let this scare you, for if the Lord should wish to test us with such sacrifices, he will grant you the graces necessary to bear them with holy courage; furthermore, you will have from them another argument to confirm you in your holy intent as one specially called and beloved by him.

In the meantime, may God bless you. Let us see to it that we aid each other with prayers and, as I leave you in the Most Sacred Heart of Jesus, I rejoice to confirm myself. (*Lett.* 102)

There are few private letters remaining to us from the period of the Pontificate, at least that have been found until now, and all are marked by the gravity of his most high ministry. However, there are also the gentle and affectionate expressions of old personal relations that reflect an image of most benevolent paternity on the figure of the Holy Pontiff. As a sample of the depth of his thoughts and the impetus of his faith, a page from the only letter to Cardinal Cavallari, his successor in Venice, to mark the dedication of the rebuilt bell tower, is sufficient:

As we read in the divine Scriptures, God speaks to us from within and from without, of himself, of his goodness and beneficence, and he speaks to us with thousands and thousands of voices that powerfully recall us to the duty of gratitude and love. To all these voices, the Catholic religion has added another, which prepares and makes straight in our heart the ways of the Lord. It is the voice of the sacred bronzes, which are washed, consecrated, and perfumed with incense and sweet aromas for this end. Invested with a high ministry, they are heralds of God's voice. They speak to us of him in all the circumstances of life, from the first infusion of grace in the soul of a child, until the day on which they announce that God himself goes from his temple to visit and console his creature, who is about to go to sleep in his bosom. As events joyful and painful rapidly follow upon each other, the sacred bells go on marking the time of prayer. Each morning, they mark the time of the Sacrifice. With greater joy each week, they announce the day of the Lord until the day when, with a melancholy sound, they invite the faithful to pray and to hope that the Christian soul be taken to Paradise on the wings of the angels.

May heaven grant that this voice will be ever heard with true fruit by the righteous, and may it call to the Lord's ways even those children who despise it because it surprises them in their wickedness and invites them, though obstinate, to conversion. (*Lett.* 291)

Therefore, this collection of letters, even in the smallness of the proportions in which it has come to us until now, gives us a new portrait of the man. Here, too, as in all the stages of his life, he knew how to unify the depth of his thoughts and intentions with the simplicity of his gestures and phrases. He always desired that his correspondents see him with that face and in the light with which they had once seen him, according to the spiritual mission that created a friendship or caused the intervention of paternal or fraternal interest and apostolic zeal. A deep prudence, a fearless determination, and an untiring zeal, which were joined together with a simplicity of gestures and a humble sense of himself, impelled him to the most unconditional dedication to the Church and to souls. That unconditional dedication makes these letters a record of rare value in contemporary Christianity, as they form an exquisite spiritual oasis, in which to hear again a most genuine echo of eternal things.

The Immaculate in the History of the World

Immaculate, maiden, pure, untouched ... in the languages of all peoples, even from the most ancient times, these are synonymous and are usually found together with "virgin." This last separates and weaves all of them into a significance that would have a recall and a consolation of supreme hope for humanity with the coming of Mary Most Holy, Virgin Mother of the Incarnate Son of God.

The Greek "parthénos"[1a]—the etymology of which is uncertain—according to the indication of the suffix—θεν—points to the swelling and flowering of life that bursts out and rises up in the surge of adolescence. Hence, within classical civilization, "virgin" indicates an exceptional stage in the manifestation of being. It is young life that flowers unblemished; it is unripe adolescence that, impetuous and laughing, bursts into the world that surrounds it. The first striking element here, strange as it may seem, is the creative energy of life, the power of the mysterious forces, which, until then, childhood had hidden within itself, as a corolla still compressed that suddenly unfolds with triumphant life. During the woman's childhood, this vital energy develops her physical being until she is on the threshold of her mission as mother. This is the mission that her heart, by secret pathways, through divine means and social indication and mission ... will have to choose. By an immediate transfer of ideas, this vital energy suggests the spiritual energy that is proper of virgins, as

---

[1] For the classical references, see Gerhard Kittel, *Theologisches Wörterbuch zum Neuen Testament*, s.v. παρθένος; vol. V (1954), p. 824 ff.

[a] See Gerhard Kittel and Gerhard Friedrich, eds., *Theological Dictionary of the New Testament*, trans. and ed. Geoffrey W. Bromiley, vol. 5, s.v. "παρθένος" (Grand Rapids, MI: Eerdmans, 1967), 826 ff.

if nature, subjugated by them, were yielding a part of its forces in the unblemished hands of those who will reserve them for the splendor of light, the triumph of flowers, the freedom of their own path through a world which, at their superhuman appearing, in part withdraws, astonished and filled with wonder. In all civilizations, "virgin" is reserved for the woman who flowers intact in her adolescence and keeps herself that way for life. Only rarely is the term applied to a man who victoriously resists the seduction of the senses, as when Euripides presents Hippolytus as a virgin soul (*Hipp.* 1006).[b] Hence, "virgin" is the "limit situation" between that of a girl who is still a child and that of a woman who has become a mother. Certainly, virginity is present in the child, but as a simple physical presence, not yet conscious, and therefore not assumed as a spiritual status, not being intimately known; it is as if it lives in dreams, in the unawareness of an unconcerned childish playfulness.

The classical world, like the Christian one, saw in unblemished youth the age and situation that most connects the creature to the divinity. The Pythia, minister of the divine oracles, is a virgin, because only a spirit free from the turmoil of the senses is a clear mirror, immediately sensible to the divine impressions (Plutarch, *Pyth. Or.* 22).[c] As we know, virgins were to be the Vestals of Rome, deputized as the custodians of the sacred fire, the symbol of the perpetuity and power of their stock. It seems as if "virginity" alone among mortals holds the privilege of direct access to the world of the divinity. On this score, many primitive legends studied by modern ethnology share the same basic mythological plot with that belabored symbol of the classical world. For example, there is the legend of "*Sabulana, the Friend of the Gods*," as it is found among the Ba-Ronga tribe of the southern Bantu. In it, the people suffered from a long famine. All of their attempts to pick the ripe fruit in the forest were in vain because, in the very act of picking the fruit, the gods who were angered would emerge from the forest, warning the men not to touch the plants. All the bold ones who dared to try to harvest some honey from a tree had their arms cut off: "One young girl remained, Sabulana. They called her, but she refused to come. . . . The oracle bones showed that Sabulana herself had to go to the sacred wood to offer a sacrifice. . . . Sabulana entered the wood and found the gods, who had all gathered together. They gave her a seat. She sat down. They greeted her and she greeted them. They said, 'How is it that you have dared to come here, and the grown-up

---

[b] Euripides, *Hippolytus* 1006.
[c] Plutarch, *De Pythiae oraculis* 22.

men have feared? What have you come for?' She answered, singing: 'I am Sabulana! I am Sabulana, the daughter of the meadow.'"[d] An innocent and unblemished daughter, she was not at all surprised to sit in such an assembly! The gods were placated. Touched, they granted her every good for her people. "Therefore, she and her mother were given the chieftainship over the whole country."[2e] There is a similar myth among the Eastern Bantu concerning a woman who obtains the fire of heaven, which the men had sought in vain to obtain.

In this limit situation, the "virgin" first hints at and then accomplishes the boldest of missions. She brings about the harshest and most poetic of realities inasmuch as she places herself on the highest elevation with regard to men and, together with them, she offers herself in the most merciful intercession and protection. The esthetical, speculative, pragmatic, and soteriological elements coincide in the virgin in a plexus of earthly and heavenly notes which, for the Greeks and Romans as for barbarians and primitives, render a fragile human creature the closest reflection of the ineffable, untouchable, resplendent, and elusive reality of the life of God. All this is present anteriorly in the symbol of the "flower," which is proper to virginity among all human civilizations, whether evolved or primitive. The flower stands between the bud, which is the first announcement of awakening life, and the fruit, which is its term and conclusion. Still enclosed, the tender bud has not yet been shaken by the impetuous buffeting of the winds, nor stimulated by the warm lure of the sun that brings life to maturity. The bud is not distinct from the branch of the tree; it is still part of the branch that bears it. On the other end, the fruit—fructifying and bearing seed—indicates the curve of the arc of life; it indicates that the whole cycle of life has been run and is moving toward its setting. The fruit, like the seed it encloses, is made for the other; it is a "being-for-the-other." It is made to be eaten and destroyed so that the life of the other may continue or so that another life may be born. Both the fruit and the bearing fruit indicate full maturity and, therefore, the conclusion of life in the implacable alternation of birth and death.

---

[2] Cf. Raffaele Pettazzoni, *Miti e leggende*, Turin 1948, vol. I, p. 65.

---

[d] English trans. from Henri Philippe Junod, *Bantu Heritage* (Johannesburg: Hortors, 1938), 129. Cf. Henri Alexandre Junod, *Les Chants et les Contes des Ba-Ronga* (Lausanne: Georges Bridel, 1897), 264–270.

[e] Junod, *Bantu Heritage*, 130.

The flower however comes from the bud, soars into infinite space, and freely sings of life. It does not decline because it does not bend toward the earth, nor does it hang heavily from a branch like a fruit, but blossoms with its corolla pointing toward the light of which it drinks as it refracts its festive colors and emanates the subtle mystery of perfumes. The flower is an object of simple contemplation and pure blessedness. Similarly, virginity, which is the flower of humanity, indicates a second birth, the divine birth possible to man and liberation from time and contingency to touch the firm immutability and incorruptibility of the spirit within one's own corporeal and visible being. What the flower, any natural flower, that is, cannot do is to arrest the transcience of its splendor in a perennial presence; this is the very thing that virginity can do in man when it is a deliberate act of the spirit. Hence, in classical mythology, Diana, the virgin, is protector of births and defender of oaths, and has the white moon as her symbol. Athena, the virgin, preserves the Palladium and incites to victory; Nemesis and Dike are also virgins who—according to Hesiod—guard the observance of law. Artemidorus says that God himself is virginal and, as intact and perpetual, flowers within his own eternal essence. To God, then, virgins and youths are particularly dear. This is the reason for the sacred character and religious function that was attributed to virginity in classical antiquity. Not only were virgins deputed for particular acts of worship, but they were also consecrated to sacrifice their lives in order to placate a wrathful divinity and to obtain protection from danger. So it was that Agamemnon sacrificed his daughter Iphigenia in order that the expedition against Troy, until then held back by contrary winds, might finally sail. Among the Hebrews, Jephthah immolated his young daughter after his victory against the Ammonites.

* * *

The mystery of "virginity," therefore, enfolds the destiny of man. Within its horizon is the hope of divine salvation that emerges for humanity insofar as virginity is considered as the means by which man ascends and approaches God and by which God descends and communicates himself to man. The concrete reality of this relationship is the concept of "virgin-mother" that is proper to revealed religion—Judeo-Christian—but which seems not to have been entirely unknown to the classical world.

Even within the classical mindset, divinity itself approaches the virgin in some way and makes her a mother. Here, symbols function in a spiritual setting, in which the poetic symbolism is perhaps less removed from the reality of the Christian dogma of the Incarnation than at first it might appear. These symbols are the light, the ray of sun, specifically the most spiritual and fertile contact that was known by the classical world. Plutarch, for example, believed that God, as spirit, could not come near or act, either in nature or in man, in any manner other than spiritual, whether as a breath, or an aura, or a ray of light.

From a moral and ascetic practice, virginity raises itself to a cosmic, soteriological principle among all civilizations that dream, think, and sing of a meeting point between heaven and earth for the salvation of man. It is through the mediation of virginity that man, burdened by the enigma of dark visions of a life prey to illness, vice, and death, seeks in the uncertain signs of the times to decipher the meaning of his own destiny. "Mother Earth" is said to be a virgin and, according to the theory of Bachofen, the religion of the mother appears to be the most ancient and diffuse form of worship. However, the cosmic mother does not allow the continuous rising up of life, if only because she is untouched and therefore continually renewing herself in her original flowering. With evidence much more resplendent than that of classical mythology, the Holy Church Fathers beginning with Tertullian call Mary untouched earth and proceeding from "earth . . . not yet deflowered by husbandry, not yet subdued by seedtime,"[f] to the "non-arable land which brought forth fruit."[g] However, in the classical mindset, the relationship "virgin-mother" was transitory and, because it was ordered toward the perpetual renewal of the fecundity of life, was not constitutive of man's relationship with the divinity.[3h] Only in the Catholic Church does the veneration of Mary become the cult of virginal maternity. In the ancient world, fecundity was much more powerful and holier than chastity. Demeter and Isis are mothers whereas Mary is Virgin and Mother. Hence, in

---

[3] Gerardus van der Leeuw, *Phénoménologie de la religion*, Paris 1948, p. 90 f.

[f] "Terra nondum opere compressa, nondum sementi subacta."
English trans. from Ernest Evans, *Tertullian's Treastise on the Incarnation* (London: SPCK, 1956), 59.

[g] "Terra non arabilis quae fructum parturiit." (*Profili di Santi* says "parturit.")
English trans. from Adam of Saint-Victor, "Salve Mater Salvatoris," in *Sequences*, trans. Juliet Mousseau, Dallas Medieval Texts and Translations, vol. 18 (Leuven: Peeters, 2013), 178–179.

[h] Cf. Gerardus van der Leeuw, *Religion in Essence and Manifestation*, trans. John Evan Turner (Princeton, NJ: Princeton University Press, 2014), 97 f.

Catholicism, monastic and priestly celibacy derive from and refer to Mary. They are sustained, protected, and beautified by her. They constitute the "angelic life" (*bios angelicòs*), which grants to the solitary man, minister of the sacraments of grace, access to the Holy of Holies and the consecration for the spiritual struggle against the opposing forces of darkness and the air.[4i]

Romantic Neoclassicism surpasses the separation of the classical meaning of "virginity" from the Christian one, which recalls maternity and the synthesis of "virgin-mother," by presenting it as an *a priori* requirement. In its catholicizing tendency, Romanticism caught a glimpse of the decisive moment of the mediation, not as a pure logical process of thought, but as a soteriological process wherein man returns to the intimacy of life with God by the path of love. Alluding to the various Christologies of Enlightenment theology, Schlegel wrote: "Christ has now been repeatedly deduced by a priori methods: but shouldn't the Madonna have as much right to be an original, eternal, and necessary ideal, if not of pure, then of male and female reason?"[5j]

Hölderlin's *Hymn to the Madonna*, which certainly belongs to his last flash of poetic activity before the year 1803, when he was struck by the darkness of folly in which this meek Titan wandered in chains for almost forty years, remains in its fragmentary state. The stanzas and pauses into which the hymn is broken are an immediate indication of the approaching storm that would overwhelm his boundless energy and render his tormented pleas for life and joy ever more futile.

> For your sake
> And your son's, O Madonna,
> I have suffered much
> Since I first heard of him
> In my tender youth;
> For the seer is not alone
> But stands under a fate
> Common to those who serve. Because I

---

[4] Cf. G. van der Leeuw, op. cit., p. 227 f.
[5] Friedrich Schlegel, *Frammenti critici e Saggi di estetica*, trans. Vittorio Santoli, no. 161, p. 83; ed. orig. *Fragmente und Ideen*, Munich and Leipzig 1905, no. 362, p. 114.

[i] Cf. van der Leeuw, *Religion in Essence and Manifestation*, 233 f.
[j] English trans. from Peter Firchow, trans., *Friedrich Schlegel's Lucinde and the Fragments* (Minneapolis: University of Minnesota Press, 1971), 195, no. 235.

> And the many songs I had
> In mind to sing to the Father
> Most High, these
> Sadness stole from me.
> . . . .
> Born from your womb
> The godly child whom
> Your kinswoman's son—named John
> By his mute father, the keen one—
> Was given the power
> Of tongue
> To interpret
>
> And the nations in terror
> The thunders and
> The rushing waters of the Lord.
> . . . .
> Above all, let the wilderness
> Be spared, divinely built
> According to pure laws, from which
> God's children have it,
> Roaming among rocks
> And the purple meadows flower
> And the dark springs
> Are for you, Madonna, and
> Your son, and for the others as well,
> Lest the gods treat them
> Like serfs, seizing what is theirs
> By force.[6k]

Here, the difficulty common to all interpretation of Hölderlin's lyric poetry is increased by the incomplete quality of a work that leaves hints and rises like a broken bow arcing into the void. The most recent exegesis of Hölderlin's work has yet to find a definitive formulation, as perhaps is also the case for his immortal colleagues and contemporaries, especially

---

[6] Friedrich Hölderlin, *Inni e Frammenti*, edited by Leone Traverso, Vallecchi, Florence 1955, p. 237 ff.

---

[k] English trans. from Friedrich Hölderlin, "An die Madonna" [To the Madonna], in *Hymns and Fragments*, trans. Richard Sieburth (Princeton: Princeton University Press, 1984), 133–139.

Schelling and Hegel. The shared environment of Tübingen, which brought them together in their youth, offered them a unitary vision of life in which man wandered about as a ruler and presaged the new age of the world raised to freedom by philosophy. A purely Greek interpretation reduces Hölderlin's Christ to a saving demigod like Heracles or Dionysus (the critic Beissner, as well as Heidegger). On the other hand, an entirely Christian interpretation (Guardini and Przywara) recognizes Christ as Son of God and Savior of the world in Hölderlin's entire corpus. A third interpretation, that of the genetic ascendant, perceives a progressive theological affirmation, which, in the works of his earliest period until *Hyperion* and *Empedocles*, is uncertain and almost drowned out by his enthusiasm for the Greek vision of life, but then becomes more pronounced—due in part to the influence of his deeply religious mother—with a growing awareness, such that the final cycle of the *Christushymnen*[7] leaves no further doubt.

Christ, the "Reconciler" (*Versöhner*), "has a place apart for himself" (*Christus aber bescheidet sich selbst*): while Hercules appears as a prince and Bacchus as the common spirit. However, Christ "is the term. Indeed, he is also of another nature, for Christ fulfills what was lacking of the divine presence in the others."[8]

Within this atmosphere of more intimate and intense recollection, of hope for the redemption of the world, as if in broken flight, move these verses "To the Madonna." Jesus is the Son, hers alone, and the Heavenly One is His Father. Christ is not reduced to an aesthetic ideal; he is a living historical reality: "Born from your womb / The godly child whom / Your kinswoman's son—named John / By his mute father, the keen one."[l] As if presaging his own painful destiny, Hölderlin looks to the Virgin immersed in her sorrowful ordeal and it is to her that he seems to turn from amidst the ominous shadows and flares that now weigh upon his spirit, oppressed by yearnings too great for a poor mortal. The fact that these lines to the Mother of God are found among the "unfinished works" of Hölderlin, the greatest lyric poet of all times, is a proof of high consolation and a symptom of the capacity of the West for spiritual renewal.

---

[7] Eduard Lachmann, *Hölderlins Christus-Hymnen*, Text und Auslegung, Herold, Wien 1951. Id., *Hölderlins Christus-Bild*, in "Stimmen der Zeit" 156, 1954–1955, p. 332 ff.

[8] Friedrich Hölderlin, *Der Einzige*, 1802: fragment of a later addition. Cf. Marianne Schultes, *Hölderlin: Christus-Welt*, Krailling vor München 1950, p. 166.

---

[l] Hölderlin, "An die Madonna," trans. Sieburth, 135

A famous example of a transcendental deduction of Mary's greatness can be read in the celebrated lectures on *The Philosophy of Art* by Schelling. Moreover, it expressly recalls the last canto of Dante's *Divine Comedy* and, like the Divine Poet, understands the function of the Virgin Mother in closest connection with the Most Holy Trinity. Schelling observes the profound difference that separates the concept of the Incarnation of God in paganism and in Christianity, because in the latter the Word of God descends into lowliness and takes the form of a servant in order to suffer or to annihilate the fallen creature in himself and reconcile it to God. The Romanticist Schelling observes that it is not easy to determine to what degree Christ is a poetical person because, unlike the Greek gods who are considered divine in spite of their finitude, he is not God in his humanity, but is true man, subject even to the suffering that is proper to humanity. It is this idea of divine suffering that suggests to Schelling the evocation of Mary:

> This same suffering and humility also characterizes the image of the *Mother of God*. Through its own inner necessity, even if perhaps not in the understanding of the *church*, it possesses symbolic meaning. It is the symbol of universal nature or of the maternal principle of all things that blooms eternally virgin. Yet in the mythology of Christianity this figure [of the virgin-mother], too, has no relationship to matter (and hence no symbolic significance); only the moral reference remains. Mary designates as archetype the feminine personage characterizing all of Christianity. The predominating factor in antiquity is the sublime, the masculine, that of modernity the beautiful and hence the feminine.[9m]

* * *

The atheist Feuerbach has delivered a polemic against such an aesthetic transposition of the classical conception of mediating femininity, which is a simple cosmic principle, into the Christian theology of the Mother of God. By antithesis, Feuerbach becomes a witness of the "sublimation" that Catholicism has worked of virginity into the cult of

---

[9] F.W.J.v. Schelling, *Philosophie der Kunst*, ed. Otto Weiss, Leipzig, Schellings Werke, vol. III, p. 81.

---

[m] English trans. from Friedrich Wilhelm Joseph von Schelling, *The Philosophy of Art*, trans. Douglas W. Stott (Minneapolis: University of Minnesota Press, 1989), 64–65.

the Mother of God. He protests against the Romantic confession that mistakes the Virgin Mother of God for a poetical ideal, which fades into the most extravagant vapors of the imagination. He accuses them of having made her the goddess of beauty, the goddess of love, the goddess of freedom of thought, the goddess of nature, and the goddess of humanity: in other words, of having turned Mary into the image of femininity, and of having dissolved the cult of the Virgin into the adoration of woman, of the eternal feminine, and of the pagan symbol of life perpetually reborn. Yet, in spite of himself, Feuerbach acknowledges that in Christianity, and above all in Catholic dogma and piety, in Mary, virginity assumes a more concrete reality that transcends all aesthetic symbols; she is chastity personified. For this reason, Mary is specifically called the model of virginity or of chastity. To serve Mary, to consecrate oneself to her, means nothing less than to forbid oneself, for love of her, every outpouring of the senses. What a difference, Feuerbach admits, between the virginity of the pagan Vestals and the virginity of Mary! Thus, Mary becomes the model of the holocaust of the senses, of the sacrifice of the flesh, of the vow of chastity for obtaining the heavenly love that consumes every earthly love. For this reason, Feuerbach concludes, in Catholic piety, the most refulgent and the most naïve titles blossom for Mary, such as only the most enflamed love can suggest.[10] In this regard, one may recall that among the early papers of Friedrich Nietzsche, the prophet of modern neo-paganism, is a large fragment from a draft of a play about the *Annunciation to Mary*, which literally follows the text of St. Luke word for word.[11] Before him, Fichte, the most profound spirit of modern idealism, had also written a sermon on the Annunciation.

It appears that in his anti-feminist recriminations, the atheist Feuerbach had in hand a pietistic counterfeit of *The Glories of Mary* by St. Alphonsus M. de Liguori. Instead, it is to this masterpiece of Catholic piety that Søren Kierkegaard turned in order to bring some warmth into the icy coldness of Reformed Christianity. His highly earnest and moving Marian texts form a welcome surprise within the gloomy heaven of Protestant piety. Kierkegaard perceives the exceptional mission of Mary in her union with Jesus, in the communion of suffering and

---

[10] Ludwig Feuerbach, *Sämmtliche Werke*, ed. Wilhelm Bolin, Stuttgart 1903, vol. VII, p. 195 ff.
[11] Friedrich Nietzsche, *Werke und Briefe*, Historisch-Kritische Gesamtausgabe, Werke I, C. H. Beck, Munich 1934, p. 221.
[Ed.] Perhaps 1933 is better.

martyrdom. This communion is focused in the Annunciation by the Angel, which initiates the mystery of the Redemption of the world in her, and in the Crucifixion, which fulfils it really in her Son and mystically in her heart as Mother of Sorrows.

Here is a meditation on the Mystery of the Annunciation from his *Journals* of 1852:

> Theme: that the angel made the right choice—for Mary made the right choice.
>
> To be sure she was the chosen one, and thus it was settled that it was she. But yet there is also a moment of freedom, of acceptance, wherein it is demonstrated that someone is the right one. If the angel had not found her such as he did find her to be, she would not have been the right one.
>
> She said: Behold, I am the handmaid of the Lord; let it be to me as you will [Lk 1:38].
>
> We are so accustomed to hearing this that we easily overlook its significance and even imagine that we would answer just this way under the same circumstances.
>
> Let us ponder on what she could—ah, far more naturally—have answered. It is good for us to ponder quite differently from the way gentle piety—not without gracefulness—has embellished this situation[n] with its own sentiments and, for example, dwelt on the thought that when the angel had spoken to Mary, it was as if the whole creation cried to Mary: O do say "Yes"! Hurry and say "Yes"! etc.
>
> She could, then—yes, as Sarah did [Gn 18:10]—she could have smiled, and she had just as good reason to. And if she could not have smiled, she could have felt herself dishonored by this salutation and dismissed it.
>
> Or she could have said: This is too exalted for me; I cannot do it; spare me, I am not up to it. The angel is clearly of the same opinion, too—that it is beyond her power. Therefore the power of the Holy Spirit must overshadow her. Well, fine, but it is precisely this, in faith to become nothing, a mere instrument—it is precisely this which goes beyond a human being's power, beyond even the utmost, utmost exertion of a person's ultimate strength. (*Diario*, 1852; II, 554)[o]

---

[n] Retained Fabro's preferred translation.
[o] *Pap.* X^4 A 454, 1852, *JP* III 2672.

The "sorrowful drama" of Mary's virginal maternity is born for Kierkegaard within the music of the angelic annunciation, precisely because of the greatness of the divine maternity that Mary receives from the Spirit and which she cannot make known to anyone, not even to Joseph her spouse. These excited reflections belong to the final pages of the *Journals* for 1854, when the life of the great Questioner of modern Protestantism, conformist and worldly, was about to be cut short.

> Yes, honor to her! O my God, when the message comes to her: You will live your life scorned by other maidens, treated as a frivolous, conceited wench or a poor, half-crazy wretch or a loose woman, and so on—after that you will be exposed to all possible suffering, and finally, because it seems as if God, too, has deceived you, a sword will pierce your heart [Lk 2:35]—this is the glad tidings.— —Yes, honor to her—to be able to say promptly, without a moment's consideration: Behold, I am the handmaid of the Lord, and then to be able to sing the song of praise: Henceforth all generations will call me blessed [Lk 1:38–48]. O my God, this is quite different from being able to speak perfectly all the living and dead languages (as our educated girls do); this is speaking in tongues [1 Cor 13:1]. (*Diario*, 1854; III, 90)[p]

Compare now the prophecy of Simeon and the extreme test of Mary's faith, of she who is fearlessly present at the death of her Son:

> "And a sword will pierce through your own soul also."
>
> Luke 2:34, 35. These parenthetical words, which were spoken in the context of the statement about Christ's being a sign which shall reveal the thoughts of many hearts, should certainly not be interpreted simply as pain at the sight of her [Mary's] son's death—no, it must be interpreted to mean that the moment, the moment of pain, the moment of agony, will come to her when, at the vision of her son's suffering, she will *doubt*—was not the whole thing a dream, a delusion, the whole affair of Gabriel being sent by God proclaiming her to be the chosen one, etc.
>
> Just as Christ cries out: My God, my God, why have you forsaken me [Mt 27:46]—so Mary must suffer through something similar on the human level.
>
> A sword will pierce through your soul—and reveal the thoughts of your heart, yours also, if you still dare believe, are still humble

---

[p] *Pap.* XI¹ A 40, 1854, *JP* III 2674.

enough to believe, that you truly are the chosen among women, the one who has found grace before God. (*Diario*, 1854; III, 92 f.)ᑫ

Lifted above the world and free of its contradictions, in a higher sphere of life and death, love and sorrow, heaven and earth, light and mystery, the Virgin Mary, who is Mother of life, of love, and of the essential light, has resolved, as the Handmaid of the Lord, who gives life to the Word, the eternal problem of salvation, which has sown anguished petitions on the pathways of human history. Poetry has never ceased collecting the enchantment of this prodigious apparition.

As a second witness, let us hear the words of Rainer Maria Rilke, neither Catholic nor Christian, at perhaps the most intense moment of lyrical ecstasy in his *Das Marien-Leben* (The Presentation in the Temple):

> But the virgin came, and lifted her eyes
> to look upon all this . . . A child.
> A little girl among women!
> Then silently she ascended
> of her superhuman strength aware
> toward the sparkling magnificence which,
> astonished, for her made way,
> so much did the cry of the Hosanna divine
> in the heart of a little child
> transcend all that men had built . . . O the immense joy,
> to abandon her to the presages within!
>
>   Her parents *imagined* they offered her
> to the Eternal One, lifting her up to Him.
> And presently to the surly priest it seemed
> that he received that tiny figure
> to his breast resplendent and bejeweled.
>
>   But the little child—small as she was—
> passed through them all like light
> so from their hands slipping
> to a destiny which higher and purer
> than the sublime hall, already was prepared
> and more solemn still than the immense Temple.[12]

---

[12] Rainer Maria Rilke, *Liriche*, trans. Vincenzo Errante, Sansoni, Florence 1947, p. 342 f.

ᑫ *Pap.* XI¹ A 45, 1854, *JP* I 364

Our third witness, Gerard Manley Hopkins, is an English poet and convert, and singer of May, the month of Mary. He sees the Virgin from within the intimacy of life's pulsation. The poem is from May 1883 and is entitled: *The Blessed Virgin compared to the Air we Breathe*—air and life, mercy and love in the mystery of Mary's universal maternity; within this mystery the deepest themes of Catholic theology are woven and developed, flowering into an intangible shiver of poetry:

> I say that we are wound
> With mercy round and round
> As if with air: the same
> Is Mary, more by name.
> She, wild web, wondrous robe,
> Mantles the guilty globe,
> Since God has let dispense
> Her prayers his providence:
> Nay, more than almoner,
> The sweet alms' self is her
> And men are meant to share
> Her life as life does air.
> If I have understood,
> She holds high motherhood
> Towards all our ghostly good
> And plays in grace her part
> About man's beating heart,
> Laying, like air's fine flood,
> The deathdance in his blood;
> Yet no part but what will
> Be Christ our Saviour still.
> Of her flesh he took flesh:
> He does take fresh and fresh,
> Though much the mystery how,
> Not flesh but spirit now
> And makes, O marvellous!
> New Nazareths in us,
> Where she shall yet conceive
> Him, morning, noon, and eve;
> New Bethlems, and he born
> There, evening, noon, and morn—
> Bethlem or Nazareth,
> Men here may draw like breath

> More Christ and baffle death;
> Who, born so, comes to be
> New self and nobler me
> In each one and each one
> More makes, when all is done,
> Both God's and Mary's Son.
> . . . .
>   Be thou then, O thou dear
> Mother, my atmosphere;
> My happier world, wherein
> To wend and meet no sin;
> Above me, round me lie
> Fronting my froward eye
> With sweet and scarless sky;
> Stir in my ears, speak there
> Of God's love, O live air,
> Of patience, penance, prayer:
> World-mothering air, air wild,
> Wound with thee, in thee isled,
> Fold home, fast fold thy child.[r]

Untouched flower, flourishing life, unripe adolescence, means of divine reconciliation, confidant and Mother of the Most High . . . after that of divinity, to which it is strictly connected, the theme of virginity is the most ancient and essential in the history of the world. It has accompanied humanity as a request for the eternal gift of visible and invisible beauty, of uncorrupt and incorruptible life, of immaculate and indefectible grace. It alone grants man the gift of absolute hope, which overcomes the distress of moments that pass and sting with remorse because those symbols of liberation and the impassioned invocations of a humanity awaiting its Savior from the Virgin Mother were no more than an anticipation of the beauty and magnificence of Mary, the Immaculate Mother of Christ. For she alone, both Virgin and Mother, was able to welcome into herself the living God and with maternal and heartrending tenderness to call "My Son!" he who was the Eternal, the Son of God.[13]

---

[13] The present text was broadcast by Radio Italiana (National Program) during the celebratory period marking the 1st Centenary of the defining of the Immaculate Conception.

---

[r] Gerard Manley Hopkins, "The Blessed Virgin compared to the Air we Breathe," in *Poems of Gerard Manley Hopkins*, ed. Robert Bridges (London: Humphrey Milford, 1918), 57–61, lines 34–72, 114–126.